The Home Office Book

The Home Office Book

DONNA PAUL

Photographs by Grey Crawford

Text Editor Bo Niles

 ARTISAN NEW YORK

Editor: Siobhán McGowan

Production Director: Hope Koturo

Published in 1996 by Artisan

A Division of Workman Publishing Company, Inc.

708 Broadway, New York, NY 10003-9555

Library of Congress Cataloging-In-Publication Data

Paul, Donna.

The Home Office Book / Donna Paul

photographs by Grey Crawford

ISBN 1-885183-30-5

1. Home offices—United States—Design.

2. Office decoration—United States.

I. Niles, Bo   II. Title.

NK2195.o4p38   1996

747.7'9—dc20

96-21064 CIP

Printed in Italy

10 9 8 7 6 5 4 3 2 1

First Printing

PAGES 2–3: **From behind antique leaded-glass windows, sunflowers greet visitors to Joanie Bernstein's office, housed within a 12-foot-high Tuscan-style tower in the middle of her home in Minneapolis. The L-shaped desktop, composed of a laminate with a sponge-painted appearance, echoes the texture of the walls. (Chapter 1, page 34)**

OPPOSITE: **Natural light streams through the 16-foot-high, wrap-around windows of Mark Edwards' San Francisco loft. His desk, an evocation of an Arts and Crafts piece, looks out over the comfortable conference area. (Chapter 3, page 84)**

CONTENTS

I began this book in Boston, where I had lived for many years. At the time, I was renting a small duplex apartment and my home office was carved out of a corner in my living room. It was, to be sure, a more "urban" home office than the one I would work in next.

The Boston apartment was only 600 square feet, so I chose to set up shop in the living room. In an attempt to make the standard desktop on file cabinets look a bit more sleek, I placed a piece of three-quarter-inch-thick glass on top of two black file cabinets. To make the corner more meaningful, I hung two paintings I had bought a few years earlier in Brazil on the wall directly ahead of me. I would occasionally gaze up at the paintings, lost in the memory of finding them, remembering the small village where I had bought them and the studio where the artist worked.

I also had two *retablos*—paintings on tin—from Mexico that held special significance for me, as well as a handmade "niche" (also from Mexico) that held objects from my travels: a doll made from rags and sticks bought from some nomadic children in the desert in Morocco, pottery from Mexico, and other odd items. These objects were treasures to me, and gave me some kind of peace and pleasure amidst the pressures of work.

My next "home" office was a small room within a charming house built in 1760 on the coast of Rhode Island, where I went with the sole purpose of writing this book. My desk was actually a pine table that was more than one hundred years old. Because it had not been designed as a desk, there were drawers that slid out from underneath the long side of the table—the exact spot where one would normally sit. The solution: I placed my computer and office chair at the short end of the table, making it perfectly workable. It also gave me a long work surface, which came in handy when spreading out papers and materials.

One tiny window framed the trees beyond. I looked out of it often. As the leaves changed color during the autumn and time meandered at a pastoral pace, I realized that not all work could be measured by a clock. What added to my contentment was the fact that I finally had my own separate work space (Private Sector/Chapter 1). It was such a treat! That the room measured only 7 by 10 feet didn't matter at all. I now knew what it was like to have my own place to work—I didn't have to share it with anyone, or have it be part of my living room.

I brought all of my "work things" (papers, folders, notebooks, etc.) with me to Rhode Island, stacking them on built-in shelves. I went to Staples and bought all sorts of file organizers to store things in. The ergonomic features of my new desk chair, the Soho chair from Knoll, instantly updated the old pine table. Setting up the fax machine took several days, however, as I couldn't find the phone jack. Turns out it was located in the basement on the other side of the house! Its wires had to be run across and up through a small hole hidden in the floor under a bookcase. Charm can have its price.

Even in this wonderful setting, I needed my personal things around me: photographs, my collection of white pottery vases, old button cards from the 1940s, my books. Their familiarity kept me company in my solitary environment.

My third home office, where I sit now, is in a pre-war building in New York City. On the ninth floor, I am blessed with unobstructed views and warm eastern light that spills across my desktop. When I first saw the apartment I knew immediately that this time my home office would go in the kitchen. At the end of the rather large (for New York City) room there was a very big window; this is where I situated my desk. Perched above the rows of trees below, looking down at my neighbors' green spaces, small balconies, and backyards, I sometimes feel as though my office is actually outside.

My present desk—a warm-toned green laminate on simple metal legs—matches the kitchen countertops. I solved the storage problem by utilizing tall bookshelves I already owned. Taking a cue from Steven Wagner (Lofty Ambitions/Chapter 3), I attached casters to the bottoms, making them mobile. Wooden blinds from Hunter Douglas create interesting shadows around the room.

Although I'm back to sharing a part of a room for my home office, having it in my favorite spot—the kitchen—makes it especially enjoyable.

I am a baby boomer. As part of the first generation that grew up with television connecting us to the rest of the world, I have come to believe that we can go anywhere and do almost anything. Since the Industrial Revolution, when people left family-owned farms and cottage industries for wage-earning jobs in factories, "going to work" has meant leaving home to go to the same company every day. Things have changed dramatically. What the Industrial Revolution pulled apart, the Information Age is pushing back together. Previous generations worked for retirement and a pension; this model just isn't viable anymore. We no longer want to punch a time clock, or count down the years to a gold watch. We plan on working longer, better, and more comfortably. Our concerns now are for environmentally and ergonomically correct homes and offices. Today's workers often have multiple careers, multiple interests, and multiple work sites.

The same generation that protested and challenged and created a social revolution in the sixties and seventies is now, in large part, responsible for another revolution, one centered around career and the workplace. Today there are millions of Americans working from home. These women and men are changing the way they approach both job and family. Indeed, they are creating a new model. They are a diverse group, comprising former executives who opt out of large corporate environments in exchange for more autonomy and a better quality of life, entrepreneurs whose sense of independence and resourcefulness have led them to this decision, and parents who are trying to combine raising children with careers that they can balance by working out of an office in the home.

The people in this book are representative of this new model. They are consultants, therapists, writers, engineers, designers, lawyers—working out of spare rooms, apartments, converted garages, basements. Their offices occupy a houseboat in Seattle's Lake Union, a Tuscan-inspired tower in Texas' famed hill country, even a tent pitched on the shores of a lake in Idaho. Their styles range from the rustic charm of country cottages to the spare lines and soaring spaces of urban lofts to the stately sophistication of New York and San Francisco town houses. These home office workers share a consciousness about space, layout, lighting, storage and design.

Finding the home offices for this book was an education: wonderfully challenging, endlessly interesting, and ultimately very inspirational. I understand more clearly now why people repeatedly spoke to me of their desire to always have personal objects nearby. To a one they rejected the standard corporate thinking that business and pleasure should never mix. From unorthodox color schemes to priceless antiques to flea-market finds, it was always fascinating for me to observe how these home owners chose to bring unexpected personal flourishes to their work spaces. My hope is that you will find both answers and ideas in these pages, as well as the inspiration to create a space of your own.

Setting aside a "room of one's own" for an office is undoubtedly the ideal scenario for anyone  who decides to work at home. A separate space offers the luxury of complete privacy and the opportunity to indulge one's idiosyncracies and personal style. Of course, standard office concerns need to be addressed, but judgment calls on storage, lighting, or the positioning of a desk can be tailored to individual quirks and habits—not the needs of a family member or business partner. No sharing + no com-promises = freedom.

And having the freedom to carve out your own space and conform to your own sched-ule is what working at home is all about.

PRIVATE SECTOR

NICK BERMAN · BRENTWOOD · CA

When Los Angeles designer Nick Berman closed his office in Santa Monica three years ago, he decided to move his business to the most convenient of locations: his home at the top of Kenter Canyon in Brentwood. The lower level of the 1971, two-story, flat-roofed house included a space he had previously ignored—a typical "rec room" of the period, complete with dark woodgrain wall panels, thick white shag carpet, and an enclosed 3-by-10-foot bar shrouded in brown plastic laminate. Once these tired materials had been removed, Nick brightened the space by painting the walls white and covering the floor in a handsome wool sisal carpet with a gridded loop pattern.

Not one to overlook an opportunity, Nick immediately recognized that, if he converted the bar into a desk-cum-drafting station, the remainder of the 400-square-foot room could be left open, providing a comfortable seating area for meetings. The bar, however, presented a problem. At 42 inches, it stood substantially higher than the average desk. If he built his desk inside the bar area at the standard height of 29 inches, his view across the room to the Pacific Ocean would be blocked. Nick's solution: raise the floor of the bar 13 inches. This not only opened up the view but also enabled him to speak with someone sitting on the opposite side of the counter. "It sounds clichéd," admits Nick, "but form followed function."

LEFT: **Wrought iron and wooden doors lead into Nick Berman's home.** RIGHT: **A comfortable seating area provides an airy place to meet with clients. The Fretwork lounge chairs in bleached oak incorporate Nick's favorite grid pattern. Matching bar stools in ebonized oak are also of his design. The fireplace, set on a slight angle and finished with integrally colored stucco, gives the space a warm and rustic feeling.**

TOP: **The converted bar is covered with two different pieces of granite: a gold/black color combination on the outside and a solid black on the inside. Low-voltage track lighting along with the Wave table lamp add a warm glow to the well-lit space.** BOTTOM: **Nick's home office allows for a desk . . . plus. The original bar extends the surface of the work area, and a slab of sleek black granite was cut to fit into a corner. The desktop rests on custom-built ebonized mahogany file cabinets. Nick's choice for seating: the Sapper Executive Chair in black leather, by Knoll.** OPPOSITE TOP: **Shelves a solid 2" thick are finished with an anigre veneer and further enlivened by playful colors of aniline dye along the facing. They fit nicely into an alcove, with room underneath for Jake the dog.** OPPOSITE BOTTOM: **Floor-to-ceiling cabinets are of plain sliced maple. Each compartment measures 24" deep and 42" wide. The door fronts are designed with Nick's trademark grid pattern and a contrasting pull of ebonized maple.**

Knowing that home offices require extensive storage space, Nick devised a variety of ways to house equipment and supplies. First, he installed a series of aniline-dyed shelves into a wall recess adjacent to the bar. Then, he flanked a new fireplace of his design with a pair of freestanding, eight-foot-high maple cabinets. The shelves offer easy access to design books and periodicals, while the cabinets provide ample room for catalogs, drawings, and fabric and paint samples.

The grid pattern of the cabinet doors not only invigorates a smooth surface but also echoes a motif Nick often introduces into many of his furnishing designs, especially chairs. In the case of his home office, the grids help de-emphasize the massiveness of the fireplace, thereby balancing the room's proportions. Set on a slight angle (one of Nick's trademarks) and finished with integrally colored stucco, the fireplace gives the space a natural, rustic feeling.

When planning the home office of her 31st-floor, two-bedroom apartment in a high-rise condominium overlooking the Chicago skyline, interior designer Terri Weinstein approached the process methodically. Conducting her initial inquiry into what she wanted as if she were carrying on a dialogue with a client, Terri asked herself specific questions, and made a list of everything that was important to her.

In designing the 11'-by-15', 165-square-foot office, Terri's goal was fourfold: Every object in the room had to have a specific place and function; everything had to be easily accessible; the space had to accommodate client meetings; and finally, the renovation had to be affordable.

As a designer, Terri gave priority to aesthetics; after all, the office would serve as her business card. To attract clients, its design had to express her signature touch: a combination of the sleek and the unexpected.

In any office, the organization of storage space is especially critical; Terri tailored hers to the specific needs of her business. For example, she is inundated with a myriad of samples, swatches, brochures, and the like—all of which take up an inordinate amount of room. Her ingenious solution to systematizing the miscellany of her showroom treks is simple and attractive: a series of gridded black plastic bins arranged across chrome Metro shelving.

ABOVE: **The clean look and smooth texture of simple plastic boxes hide the inevitable jumble of any office. The boxes measure 12" x 18" and function as carryalls, holding books, wood samples, and fabric swatches. Side by side on Metro shelving, they slide out for easy access.**

RIGHT: **Terri's desk is a paean to pure form. Two contrasting geometric shapes intersect boldly: the round section swivels to form an expanded work surface or an instant conference table. The desk is from the TAO collection made by Davis Furniture.**

Terri's desk is constructed like a three-sectioned stabile. The base, containing a set of drawers for extra storage, supports two work surfaces: a cantilevered circle of natural sycamore which serves as a conference table, and an asymmetrical beech wedge, stained a deep purple, where Terri works. The wedge ells alongside the window wall to connect with a counter running along the wall behind the desk, creating a generous work space—not to mention a visually dramatic effect.

In addition to her busy practice, Terri teaches design and lighting at the Art Institute of Chicago, so she was aware of the critical part correct lighting plays in office comfort. South light streams into her office through a large wall of windows, complemented by track lighting, a desk lamp, and a string of half-inch Invizilite halogen bulbs installed under the wall cabinets behind her desk.

The wall itself is banked with storage options, including a series of lateral files topped by a counter and open shelving above for Terri's ever-growing collection of international design magazines and specifications books. The counter and the wallboard behind offer plenty of room for assembling paint and fabric swatches and other materials for her clients' consideration.

OPPOSITE TOP: **An ebonized wood filing cabinet is the third geometric module in the TAO desk. Not only the shapes contrast, but the colors do as well: the surface sections are of natural sycamore and purple-stained beech.** OPPOSITE BOTTOM: **A wall beneath shelves is the perfect staging area for paint and fabric samples. To provide a good surface for pins and tacks, it is covered with cotton duck fabric. The Invizilite system of halogen bulbs provide the neutral light essential for making color choices.** RIGHT: **Using every bit of available space, Terri filled a small area to the edges with custom-built flat files finished in black lacquer. Large drawers allow easy viewing of oversized samples of tile, glass, stone, etc.**

Terri's home office expresses her signature style: a combination of the sleek and the unexpected.

LEFT: **Frederieke Taylor's prewar residential building in Greenwich Village.** BELOW: **The steel beams allow the desk to be cantilevered out over the living room.** OPPOSITE: **The apartment functions on two levels— the living room below and the loft-like office above.**

Although the home office of art consultant Frederieke Taylor appears to be open to the rest of the apartment, it is in fact a private space. A space she refers to as her "hideaway, high above the living room."

When she purchased the cooperative apartment in one of the fine old residential buildings in Greenwich Village, she was captivated by the 18-foot vaulted ceiling embellished with plaster detail. At that time, she was working with the curators of the Museum of Modern Art to coordinate the Deconstructivist Architecture exhibition. Her background in the arts and her knowledge of architecture led her to the innovative design team of Smith-Miller + Hawkinson Architects for her own renovation.

The first thing they did was open up the space on the upper level—"to create a command post for her to work from," explains Laurie Hawkinson. The architects felt that if Frederieke was going to be working from home, they wanted to design a space which "would very much put her in control." They also took into consideration her extensive art collection, convinced that she should be visually connected to it when working.

ABOVE: The steel beam was left unfinished for an industrial look mirrored in the decor of the office. Along the railing, a sheet of Lexan—a sandblasted Plexiglas material—adds its own textured sleekness.

RIGHT: The gently arched ceiling is rather low over the desk, but the expanse of windows below compensates. A black metal floor has holes for a sense of airiness and surprise. The easy comfort of an old wicker chair provides counterpoint to the industrial architectural materials.

The team began by uncovering an original staircase, previously hidden, that allowed access to the upper level. It was here that Frederieke could receive clients and review their artwork. Since this room was separate from the rest of the apartment, it was clearly the place to build an office.

By utilizing the double-height space with its vaulted ceiling and by extending the cantilevered desk out over the living room, Frederieke was able to take advantage of a view directly facing an 18-foot-high wall of windows. Constructing the desk of sandblasted Lexan (a high strength Plexiglas) and perforated metal allowed for a sense of unexpected lightness.

The space behind the desk is big enough to accommodate a sitting area and a large flat file that doubles as a table. Along one wall are sliding perforated-aluminum doors that conceal art storage and shelves for papers and books.

When work is in progress, the perforated-aluminum doors slide open to reveal books, office materials, and art. The color of the doors is neutral so as not to compete with artworks, but the warm finish gives the room a satiny texture. Oversized flat files provide not only storage but also a large table space: the galvanized metal top complements the aluminum on the walls.

When Thomas Callaway, an architectural and furniture designer, bought his Spanish Colonial Rancho-style house on a quiet street in the Brentwood section of Los Angeles, he had a vision: to transform the dwelling, originally built in 1928, into a re-creation of another place and time. Describing the inspiration behind his design, Tom explains, "The concept for my home office came from artist studios built in New Mexico in the '20s and '30s. They were tiny, charming spaces. I always yearned to have something with that kind of character for myself."

Tom's affection for the Spanish Colonial vernacular style peculiar to many Southern California communities is palpably evident in his meticulous and sympathetic renovation—especially of his new home office. The office occupies a private, 15'-by-30', 300-square-foot sanctuary at the back of the second story of his house and opens to a narrow, brick-paved balcony overlooking a leafy courtyard and pool. Other than the ringing of the telephone and fax machine, the only sounds to be heard are the chirping of birds and the bubbling of water out of a fountain into the pool.

LEFT: **Lush foliage surrounds the entrance to Tom's house.** BELOW: **Tom's new office wing as seen from the pool area.** RIGHT: **The entrance to the office is marked by two old wooden columns from Mexico.**

TOP: **By building a small balcony overlooking the courtyard, Tom can open the doors to trees, gentle breezes, and the sound of falling water.** BOTTOM: **Tom salvaged and painted old wood to make doors for the storage closet and cabinet above the small sink. An antique bookshelf from Mexico incorporates two cultures with its Spanish-Moorish arches and rustic Indian decorations. Tom left the piece just as he found it, with its worn and faded patina.** RIGHT: **Tom's office resembles a one-room cabin somewhere in New Mexico. While a leather and fabric armchair and the** *kiva* **fireplace are inviting, the work area is strictly business. It was made of two basic storage units topped with a plank of laminated plywood.**

Storage throughout the room is eclectic yet inventive and purposeful, varying from a hand-molded adobe-style bookcase to vinyl-coated wire pull-out shelves to a painted wood carryall used to store rolled drawings and papers. Tom assembled the desk from a laminated plywood top and storage units purchased at an office supply store. Lighting is supplied by a series of spots recessed into the ceiling between the *vigas*. At night, a desk lamp and the glow from the flames in the *kiva* lend an atmosphere of warmth.

Two tapered columns imported from Mexico stand at the entrance to the room. Inside, walls faced with plaster resemble adobe, and the ceiling is punctuated by massive, rounded, hand-hewn beams called *vigas*. A classic Southwestern *kiva*, or molded-plaster fireplace, occupies one corner of the room. Closet doors reconfigured by Tom from weathered wood reflect what he terms the "territorial Mexican" mode.

ABOVE: **The "Nina" chair shown here is from Tom's furniture line. The bones were found on one of his many trips to the desert.** RIGHT: **Slide-out plastic organizers expand the space of a narrow cabinet.** OPPOSITE: **Modern meets primitive: the fax machine sits on an antique Mexican table in front of adobe-style bookshelves.**

Joanie Bernstein's home office in the Golden Valley section of Minneapolis seems to radiate golden light and hum with good vibrations. This atmosphere is a reflection of Joanie herself, an upbeat, high-energy, artist's representative.

Several years ago, when Joanie and her husband, artist/illustrator Jack Molloy, were expecting their son Zach, they decided to move into a larger, all-new house. To plan the exact location of Joanie's home office, they hired architect Blake Bichanich. Joanie wanted a spot that would be accessible to general household activities, but with a vantage point from which she could monitor the comings and goings of the messengers delivering her artists' portfolios. For this practical reason, Bichanich positioned the office in a 12'-by-15', 80-square-foot balcony overlooking the front entrance.

After a year, though, Joanie found the loft-like office too open and noisy; she realized that in order to concentrate on her work, she needed more privacy. Jack came up with the perfect solution: he would build her a tower.

At Architectural Antiques, an emporium dedicated to salvaging artifacts from old houses, the couple dis-

covered a set of antique leaded-glass windows which had originally adorned a garden room in a nineteenth-century mansion in the city. To encase the windows, Jack built the walls of Joanie's office up 12 feet, then troweled their surface with a thick, textural coating of plaster. Sponge-painting the walls a warm, sunny yellow ensured that, although it was now enclosed, the space would always feel glowing and cheerful, even on the dreariest Minnesota winter day.

ABOVE: **A world within a world: Jack built a 12-foot-high Tuscan-style tower in the middle of the house to serve as Joanie's office. The outside was designed "to feel like a downtown alleyway." An important aspect of this plan is the clear separation between work and domestic life.** RIGHT: **Joanie's Techline desk is an L-shape, with the short end designated for storage, phone, and a genuine typewriter. Overhead cabinets include open cubbyholes for easy access to envelopes and stationery.**

Joanie custom-designed her own work surface and storage, combining elements from the Techline Home Office System. Playing off the amber hues of the walls, she chose modular wall and base cabinets of red oak. An L-shaped desktop, composed of a laminate with a sponge-painted appearance, echoes the texture of the tower. One branch of the "L" rests on a base made from a column that was cut in half; the other stretches across a pair of cabinets devoted to drawers and files. The Techline System works well for Joanie because she is "drawn to the wide open space of the desktop." But the aspects of the office that most captivate her are the interior windows and the elevated position. "It feels so much like a tree house," she says, "and it's filled with light every day of the year."

LEFT: **Large windows separate the office from the rest of the house. Made of leaded glass, they impart an exotic richness.**
RIGHT TOP: **Joanie represents illustrators—including her husband, Jack Molloy. Here, one of his handmade paper journals sits by the fax machine. The handy ledge built on the back wall is useful for propping up postcards and brochures.**
RIGHT BOTTOM: **A vaulted bookcase set into molded plaster.**

Rare is the home with so many rooms that one can be dedicated to a totally private office. More commonly, the room chosen for that purpose must perform a multitude of functions. Some offices tuck into a corner of a living room, dining room, or study, while others take over a spare closet. Many double as guest rooms.

Careful planning is critical in establishing a multifunctional home office, so that the space can feel equally comfortable in each of **QUICK-CHANGE ARTISTS** its guises. The cleverest offices prove that flexibility and style are indeed compatible, even if the solutions, on occasion, surprise.

QUICK-CHANGE ARTISTS

Beyond the sliding wooden doors of Henrietta's office is her own private space.
OPPOSITE: **Henrietta's home office and guest room as seen from the living room.**

HENRIETTA GWALTNEY · NEW YORK

In 1994, Henrietta Gwaltney, a successful family psychotherapist, decided to combine her interpersonal skills with her love of art. Without dissolving her therapy practice of 25 years, she founded Quintessential New York, a company that leads behind-the-scenes tours of the city's studios and galleries. Explaining this unusual pairing of endeavors, she says, "I have always helped people try to get what they want out of life, so now I guide some of them in a more literal way—by providing them with a special and unique experience of the city."

To handle these two demanding jobs, Henrietta needed a home office as flexible as she is. Her office would not only have to perform double duty for the two separate businesses but would also have to function, on occasion, as a comfortable guest room—and as an extension of her living room when necessary.

Henrietta turned to Clodagh, a New York designer best known for spare, flexible interiors attuned to the harmonies that exist in nature. Color, texture, light, and sound are her "pathways" to peaceful, holistic environments that quietly smooth out the rough edges of daily life.

Clodagh has a penchant for designing rooms that can function in a number of ways. "In an ideal world," she muses, "we would have separate spaces for everything, but, when we don't, I use magical tricks to make spaces appear different." In Henrietta's apartment, Clodagh's magic relies on the sleight-of-hand of sliding screens and walls.

To give the impression of a private entrance for clients arriving at Henrietta's third-floor, two-bedroom apartment in a postwar high-rise, Clodagh replaced standard walls with Japanese-style shoji screens, which she then angled to lead the visitor into the office just to the left of the front door. Shojis, being translucent, afford a sense of privacy, yet also amplify the sense of space, because they allow ambient light to pass through. At night, when lit from behind, they glow like lanterns.

For convenience, Henrietta's office occupies the first room off the entrance hall, and it also adjoins her living room. Sliding walls, like magical updates of old-fashioned pocket doors, separate the two spaces. Ingeniously, they conceal storage cabinets and computer equipment when open.

A copper planter extends eight feet along the windowsill behind the desk to "bring nature in and push the sounds of the street back." Diaphanous linen shades "veil" the windows, enhancing the feeling of quiet seclusion.

In the entrance hall, elegant shoji screens keep the bedroom hidden from view when clients and guests arrive. Elizabeth Jackson designed the leaf-patterned rug.

LEFT: **A built-in desk of birch plywood runs the length of the office's window wall. To the right of the desk, a door slides open to reveal an additional storage compartment containing computer equipment.**
ABOVE: **A sofa bed upholstered in rich purple fabric and decorated with embroidered and damask pillows gives the space a luxurious feel.** RIGHT: **The modern version of a traditional wing chair, on wheels.**

The serenity of the warm-toned office, coupled with Henrietta's calm disposition, creates a soothing atmosphere, perfect for a therapy session or a business meeting. Friends who happen to stay overnight benefit, too, from Henrietta's nurturing temperament; Clodagh custom-designed a sofa that pulls out into a commodious trundle bed. The sofa bed is covered in aged, crushed velvet, in a copacetic color the designer calls "Concord Grape."

Pillows made of Banjara embroideries from the mountains of central India decorate the reception area of Antonio's home office. RIGHT: Storage cabinet and wall are painted in hues of green; doors are black and seafoam yellow, framed by sage gray. Postcards, invitations, and art announcements add to the vivid mélange.

A native of Bahia, Brazil, Antonio Da Motta Leal now lives in New York City, where he works as a stage designer for both theater and film. His home and office reflect his sense of drama as well as his affinity with exotic cultures, including that of his homeland. Objects such as masks, fabrics, and carvings collected on his travels invest his home office with an atmosphere of mystery.

In planning how he could live and work out of the same space—a 750-square-foot, one-bedroom apartment in a prewar building formerly used for industrial purposes—Antonio was aware that he would have to reserve one of the three rooms for multiple functions. He needed adequate space to carry on his business but did not want to relinquish pleasant surroundings in which to relax and entertain.

Antonio established a focal point at one end of his living room with one of two matching 8-by-10 sisal rugs banded in coffee-brown canvas, on which he set an exquisite 19th-century Biedermeier desk from Germany. By demarcating the space in this manner, Antonio set the tone for the entire room. By day, the burled-walnut desk is ideal for laying out his interior and furniture designs; by night, its high-gloss polished top can be used as a serving station for parties.

Because he does not own his apartment, Antonio designed a row of long, low, birch plywood cabinets that can be disassembled and moved, if and when he does. An existing boxed-in duct and a structural column, now hidden behind a tall bookcase, stand at either end to frame the modular cabinets. On the wall between the two, Antonio suspended a series of glass shelves to showcase miniature prototypes of his best-known furniture designs as well as objects he has collected from all over the world. He framed the wall under the lowest shelf with cork so that invitations, notices of upcoming events, and current memos could be pinned up for his instant inspection.

The base cabinets conceal storage, including a two-drawer file cabinet for correspondence, a flat file for drawings, shallow drawers for office supplies, and shelves for additional books, papers, and a stereo and CD collection. Two separate, side-by-side sliding shelves pull out when Antonio needs a second surface to showcase drawings.

Another, freestanding cabinet that Antonio designed and constructed from walnut and cedrino, an Amazonian wood, holds stationery and his company brochures. By positioning this cabinet in front of the flowing muslin curtains shielding his windows, Antonio emphasizes its sculptural qualities and inherent visual drama.

Masks made by the Guarany Indians sit above a file cabinet. RIGHT: **Basic wooden cabinets contain hanging files, slatted drawers, and a pull-out shelf.**

One of Antonio's favorite pieces of furniture is his "Asmodel" lidded stool, which he designed to emulate those used by North African nomads for transporting goods and guarding treasures. The lid lifts off to reveal a deep storage cavity within its base.

While fully aware that his office appears unusual, Antonio feels that "it reflects my true nature—I need these objects from all over the world around me when I work. They help me to think, create, be free."

OPPOSITE: **Using traditional methods of 17th-century marquetry, Antonio designed the Ratziel cabinet. Bronze-cast knobs were fashioned from Amazonian nuts. The cabinet springs to life when its doors are opened.**

LEFT AND ABOVE: **The 21-inch-deep "Asmodel" lidded stool stores files, phone books, and papers. A range of African fabrics cover the seats of the stool. Kuba cloth, also from Africa, gives an organic dimension to the cobalt-blue wall.**

Life in a small condominium can be a challenge—whether or not one works at home. Space for extra, unanticipated needs is often limited, as it was in Stephen Gibson's 900-square-foot, City-Row-House-style home in San Jose, California.

Stephen's job as a corporate management consultant requires him to work from home. A former painter and illustrator, he also enjoys making furniture from wood salvaged from antique chests and tables. Stephen wanted to designate a private zone to overnight guests, but because he could not add an office, a "wood shop," and a guest bedroom to his condominium, he reconfigured one end of his soaring 15-by-25-foot living room to serve all three purposes.

Structurally, the decision of where to place the office/workshop/bedroom was predetermined by the existence of an 11-by-12-foot alcove within the L-shaped room. To create a separation between the alcove and the larger space, Stephen, an admirer and collector of Asian art and artifacts, collaborated with a Japanese craftsman to custom-design a flexible partition of translucent shoji screens. Although the room rises to

Custom-designed shoji screens act as a translucent wall within Stephen's L-shaped living room. RIGHT: Screens open to reveal the office/wood shop/guest room. The kanji characters on the scroll translate into English as "bright and shining."

LEFT: **Linen curtains hung from a simple copper pipe conceal the wood shop which occupies a corner of the office. Panels of gauze dyed a copper color to resemble wooden molding encircle the room.** RIGHT: **To maximize the space, Stephen took advantage of the 20-foot-high ceilings. By placing objects he treasures in a visible spot above the closets, he can appreciate them out of the way of the "work space."**

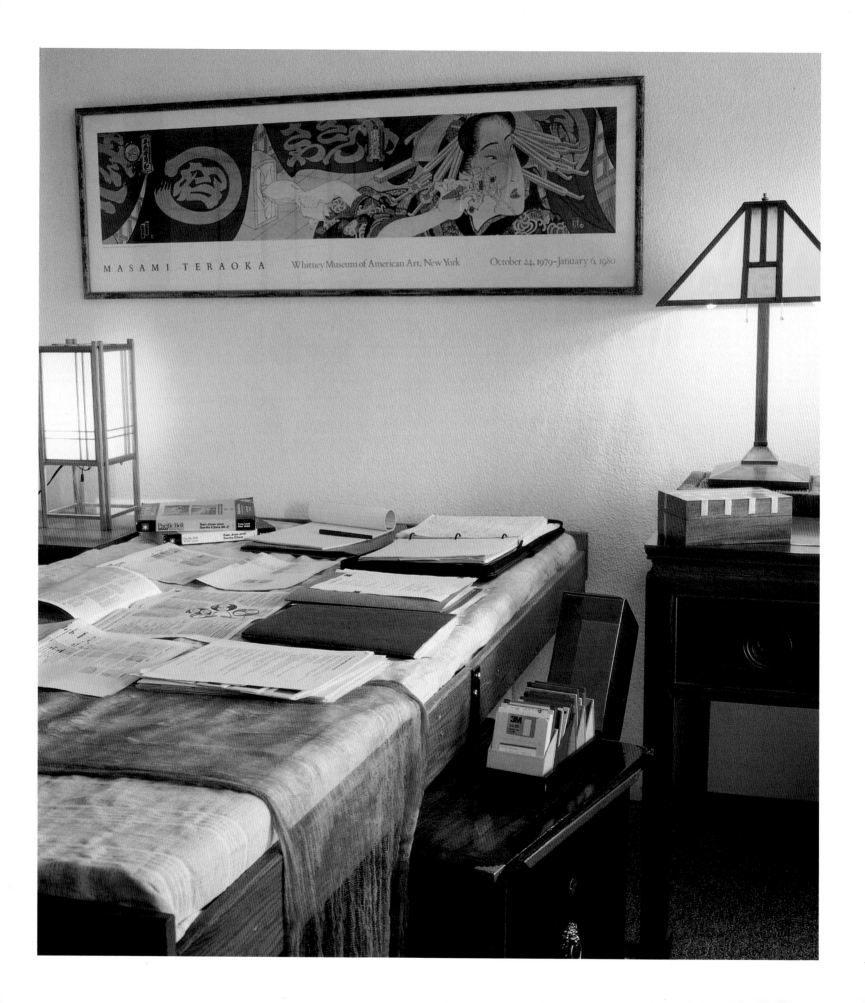

a 20-foot-high pitched ceiling, Stephen maintained a standard wall height of eight feet for the sliding screens. This enhances the open, airy mood of the room and allows light from a large fan-shaped window set into the inverted "V" of the roof to spill into both spaces. A band of copper-colored gauze runs along two walls of the alcove at the same height.

Stephen equates living and working in a multipurpose room with living on a boat, because the combination of limited space and multiple needs forces one to be orderly—and inventive. When pressed for space to spread out papers, for example, Stephen turns the top of his guest bed into a work surface; he positions the bed right next to his desk so that he can pivot his chair and move from one surface to the other with ease. He also designed and constructed several storage chests to slide under the bed, and one to double as a bedside table.

An 8-by-3-foot section of the office is reserved for the workshop. Situated by the window, and behind one of the shoji panels, it is all but invisible from the main part of the living room. Flowing tab-top linen panels suspended from copper tubing pull across to conceal any mess or work-in-progress.

LEFT: **The futon bed's hard, flat surface is useful for spreading out materials when Stephen is working on a large project. To the right, a Mission-inspired desk lamp is paired with a Japanese paper lamp.** RIGHT TOP: **A group of** *tansus* **includes a stacked antique Japanese example and a smaller chest with drawers that Stephen made.** RIGHT BOTTOM: **Stephen reconfigured this small cabinet with a sliding door. It slips under the bed when not in use.**

Karen Fisher doesn't like to leave New York. In fact, her favorite place to be is her own apartment. And why not? Although it encompasses a mere 500 square feet, her one-bedroom home on the penthouse floor of a 1907 building feels like an aerie, with its spectacular views of Manhattan rooftops and a verdant 400-square-foot wraparound terrace.

Karen founded and runs Designer Previews, a consulting company that matches interior designers to potential clients. Her business gives her access to New York's top talents, so one evening, over sushi, she casually asked Clodagh, whose creative and flexible approach to space appealed to her personal sensibility, to evaluate her apartment and her needs. Clodagh responded with an ingenious plan for Karen's living room that completely transformed the space, causing it to seem twice its size.

Because one of Clodagh's hallmarks is her incorporation of natural elements in interior design, the first thing she did was open up the living room to the wraparound terrace, so that, when desired, inside and out would feel as one. A step-through long window casts plenty of daylight on the new work zone, and honey-toned sisal carpeting fuses with the

LEFT: **Karen's office is situated in the penthouse apartment of a venerable building overlooking Manhattan's historic Gramercy Park, a private square in the middle of the city.** BELOW: **Not all offices are indoors. As much as possible, Karen brings her work outside to her terrace.** RIGHT: **The oval dining table doubles as a confererence space when Karen meets with clients. Clodagh created the piece using an old Viennese pedestal as the base and adding the top.**

parchment-hued walls to amplify the ambient light and enhance the tranquil mood.

The second trick was to get organized. Clodagh recalls that when she first saw Karen's apartment, "there was stuff everywhere." Her solution was to turn one living-room wall into a closet, which now contains Karen's home office. Although it measures a compact 8-by-2½ feet, the space contains every-

ABOVE: **Folding doors let Karen's home office go from zero to sixty in seconds. When closed, they give no hint of the business nerve center beyond. Guests see only an elegant living room.** RIGHT: **With doors open, the compact office is home to computer, fax, and multiple storage compartments. A portable printer stand slides under the desk when not in use. The black leather easy chair is by Montis.**

thing Karen needs to run her business efficiently and effectively. Clodagh's design also allows Karen use of the entire room and terrace when she's not working. In fact, the room adjusts perfectly to parties.

By utilizing what she calls "slices of wall" in many of her installations, Clodagh effectively plays hide-and-seek with storage spaces where they don't seem to exist. Karen's living room is a case in point: when the 8$\frac{1}{2}$-foot, floor-to-ceiling, faux-painted wooden bi-folds in front of the office are closed, they look like a solid, paneled wall. But when they part, all is revealed. Shallow drawers, neatly partitioned bookcases, a pull-out shelf for the computer keyboard—everything Karen needs is at her fingertips.

A built-in banquette along the opposite, windowed end of the room serves as seating for clients when Karen makes presentations, which she does at a pedestal table created from an antique Viennese base combined with a new metal top made to look like wood. When not in use for business purposes, this end of the room is a cozy and inviting venue for dinner parties.

OPPOSITE: **Vertical compartments keep files, papers, and miscellaneous items organized. Work surfaces slide out at several levels. A spacious keyboard shelf extends the full width of the desk.** ABOVE: **Floor-to-ceiling shelves within a shallow cupboard provide a bonus storage space.** LEFT: **The keyboard shelf disappears when not in use. Inside drawers, papers are arranged in a metal organizer.**

Katina Arts Meyer's tiny, charming home office is so versatile that she is able to transform it into an intimate dining room in a matter of seconds. Located in one of New York City's most magical buildings, the 1917 Hotel des Artistes, the 10'-by-6', 60-square-foot office appears quite precious at first glance, but it is truly built to—and for—work.

Katina, a teacher in the decorative arts graduate program at the National Design Museum (formerly the Cooper-Hewitt) and at the Parsons School of Design, is also a practicing interior designer. Her background in art history and her passion for the decorative arts have blessed her with the ability to mix antiques with high tech in a personal and inventive way.

LEFT: **Wooden floors painted in a diamond pattern lead into the office.** ABOVE: **Katina's work surface folds down from the wall like a Murphy bed. The shelf is large enough to accommodate her fax, laptop computer, papers, and reference books. A treasured antique chair is her choice for seating.**

Knowing she needed to house a computer, fax, television, stereo system, and sizable collection of books in a fairly small space, Katina devised two walls of built-in bookcases and cabinets to contain them. Her elegant and unique solution for cabinet doors was easy and inexpensive: she installed shirred panels of linen gauze behind framed "panes" of brass mesh. The look is lighter and airier than plain, solid doors—

Linen panels framed with mesh screen conceal Katina's working library. To the right, the professional woman's version of the old-fashioned telephone table.

Tea is served: the perfect setting for an afternoon meeting.
OPPOSITE: **Shirred curtain doors open to reveal four large file cabinets.**

"very French," according to Katina. The refined panels are also practical; by attaching Velcro strips to frame and fabric, she can remove and launder the panels when necessary.

To create an illusion of spaciousness and link the office to the rest of the four-room apartment, Katina color-washed the hardwood floors in a seafoam green and white checkerboard pattern. Antique leaded-glass doors, formerly a pair of old windows dating from the same period as the Hotel des Artistes, separate the work area from her bedroom.

Katina likes to spread out her work over several surfaces. One of these is a delicate antique Sheraton mahogany folding game table, which is paired with a 19th-century Anglo-Indian chair given to her by her mother. Another is an 18-by-30-inch shelf, tucked into a specially designed niche, that pulls down and away from the center of the main book wall. When raised, the shelf hides the computer and its companion printer.

As there is no available natural light in the room, Katina recessed three halogen spotlights into the ceiling. They provide plenty of light for working. In the evening, when she entertains, she dims them and brings in candles for atmosphere.

The open space, majestic height, and abundant light that charac-

terize the typical loft can prove inspirational when considering how to incorporate a home office into its overall plan. For many loft-dwellers, how-ever, a primary concern is how to mesh domestic and professional life. Indeed, sep-arating home and office in such a vast space presents a specific challenge: how to suc-

cessfully establish a personal area for fam-

ily life while ensuring privacy at work. To

this end, unusual materials take on a new

meaning as they adapt

to myriad functions. Loft living, in sum, offers

an opportunity to work with the archi-

tectural equivalent

of a blank canvas.

CHAPTER 3

LOFTY AMBITIONS

WONG / STROUD · BOSTON

When architect Janine Wong began designing the 1,650-square-foot loft she shares with her husband, Jim Stroud, and their son, Ryder, in an early 20th-century industrial building in Boston's Fort Point Channel area, she knew the space had to meet several demands. A design professor at the University of Massachusetts who had spent years with large architectural firms, Janine wanted to work from home so that she could spend more time with Ryder. Jim, a print publisher for many Boston and New York artists, wanted to hold gallery openings at the loft to exhibit clients' portfolios.

Aware that she had room to build upward but no excess floor space, Janine devised an ingenious plan to keep the scale large and open in her home office. She took a 10-foot-long portion of the wall at the end of the living area and constructed a pair of side-by-side closets, each two feet deep and five feet wide. At 12 feet, the closet doors rise to the full height of the ceiling. Due to invisible hinges, the doors appear to be seamless panels when closed, creating a dramatic backdrop for a portfolio of prints by artist James Hanson, with whom Jim collaborated on the production of the plates.

To play with the idea of pictures and frames, and to set apart the office area, Janine designed a large, free-form frame around the entire closet. The frame, made of mahogany, is stained with four different pigments (sienna, ocher, yellow, and green) to reveal the grain of the wood. Upon entering the loft, one is instantly drawn to this "frame within a frame."

LEFT: **The left side of the paneled wall conceals Janine's library of art and design books as well as a stereo.** RIGHT: **The right side of the wall contains a complete home office with filing cabinets, shelves, and computer.**

LEFT: **Twelve prints by artist James Hanson are mounted in identical gold frames. The irregular shapes and contrasting color stains of the asymmetrical door frames produce a substantial yet whimsical effect.**
RIGHT TOP: **Everything has its place within the small area. A fan next to the computer circulates air. A piece of laminate placed across the top drawer of the slide cabinet makes a handy surface for the mouse pad. A conventional file cabinet fits easily under the shelf.**
BOTTOM: **The work table by the window benefits from an abundance of natural light—perfect for painting.**

The closet doors—and the cabinets they conceal— are built on two levels. The lower cabinets, which Janine refers to as "active space," hold the primary elements of the office. The upper ones store items she needs less often. One of the lower cabinets houses a library of books plus stereo equipment. The other is for the office proper, containing computer, printer, storage, and shelving. When the doors are open, Janine simply pulls her office chair out into the loft.

A SoHo building is home to Dan Miller and his graphic design business. BELOW: Two bird's-eye maple tables with black lacquer legs support three computer workstations. The area is separated from the living room by a row of storage cabinets. An elongated print by Nancy Spero makes a colorful coun-

terpoint to the computers. OPPOSITE: **During off-hours a row of copper mesh screens stands on top of the storage cabinets. The computers are still visible, but almost as a mirage. A Jennifer Convertibles' sofa is dressed up with pillows made from antique Japanese kimono fabric.**

When Manhattan-based graphic designer Dan Miller decided to move his office to his 2,000-square-foot SoHo loft, the first thing he did was hire William Sofield and Thomas O'Brien of Aero Design Studio to mastermind the organization of his space. Dan, who describes his taste as International Style with a hint of the Japanese and some '50s furniture thrown in, knew he could trust the Aero pair to adapt his quirky sensibility to a functional environment.

To separate Dan's home from his office, Bill and Thomas erected a series of translucent glass panels framed in teak across the kitchen/bedroom area. During the work day, the panels slide closed, sealing off Dan's personal space.

The open-plan living room/work area/conference room covers about 1,000 square feet. Two bird's-eye maple tables with black-lacquered legs, extending a total of 14 feet across, stand against one long wall; on these Dan set up three computer workstations, for himself and his assistants. To create an aisle parallel to the tables and to separate the office from the living room and conference area, Bill and Thomas designed a series of 28-inch-high modular cabinets, made of pickled particleboard with solid cherry trim. These store books, papers, and office supplies. During the day, the seating area provides a comfortable space to meet with clients. In the evening, when Dan wants to

Workstations and living area
co-exist within the main room
of the loft.

entertain, he places folding copper mesh panels on top of the low cabinets to mask the view of the office. Lit from behind, the copper mesh casts a warm glow over the entire loft.

Because storage is a major concern in a space as open as Dan's, he utilized every conceivable option —even the kitchen and bathroom. In custom-blackened steel cabinets next to his fireplace, vertical files hold drawings and design boards. Beneath the marble top of the work island in the kitchen are shallow flat files for sketches, catalog layouts, and other oversized work. And in a corner of a small bathroom sits the photocopier, placed there because Dan regards it as one of the more unsightly pieces of office equipment ever designed.

OPPOSITE BOTTOM LEFT:
To keep the photocopier out of sight, Dan found a home for it next to the marble pedestal sink in the bathroom.
OPPOSITE RIGHT: **Along an original brick wall, cabinetry constructed in blackened steel accommodates vertical storage, stereo, and fireplace. Pony skin gives a new twist to that modern icon, the Eames chair.**
RIGHT: **Even in the kitchen, work is never far away: a marble-topped island doubles as a flat-file cabinet.**

The old Jackson Brewery building in San Francisco's loft district. RIGHT: **The clean lines of a custom-made table by Berkeley Mills sets the tone in Mark's loft, while a four-compartment display shelf gives character to the cool white wall. Draped muslin softens the light from the 17-foot-high windows, and a lantern-like sconce welcomes visitors to the office.**

Two years ago Mark Edwards changed his life. He left his job at a national consulting firm to start his own company creating compensation programs for high-tech organizations. Needless to say, he needed a new place to work.

Mark purchased a huge 2,500-square-foot loft with 17-foot-high ceilings in the old Jackson Brewery building in San Francisco's hip SoMa (South of Market) area. Although he initially planned to use this space only for work, he found himself spending more and more time there. He grew to like it so much that he decided to live there too.

With a corner position and natural light streaming through 16-foot-high wraparound windows, the loft had great potential, but planning how to best use the space was new to Mark. He was, however, clear about one thing: he wanted the office to be the central point of his home.

With this in mind, Mark had a stepped *tansu* chest made for the open area under the stair leading to the upper level of the loft. The piece was created by Berkeley Mills, a company that specializes in designing and manufacturing custom Arts and Crafts and Asian furniture through use of a special software program. On the computer, the team was able to modify fea-

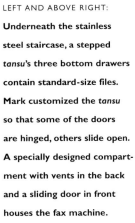

LEFT AND ABOVE RIGHT:
Underneath the stainless steel staircase, a stepped *tansu*'s three bottom drawers contain standard-size files. Mark customized the *tansu* so that some of the doors are hinged, others slide open. A specially designed compartment with vents in the back and a sliding door in front houses the fax machine.

tures of the *tansu* to Mark's specifications so that he could visualize the chest in the context of his loft prior to its being built.

Mark's *tansu*, crafted of mahogany with maple trim, provides a total of 14 feet of lateral file space, as well as numerous other cubbies of varying sizes, including one engineered specifically for the fax, with vents in the wood for air circulation.

Mark positioned his desk, an evocation of an Arts and Crafts piece, in the middle of the living area of his loft, in front of the stair and the *tansu*. An over-sized, overstuffed sofa, two cushy chairs, and a low stone coffee table on big rubber wheels are the only other appointments in the space—just enough for a meeting, just enough for home-alone comfort.

Steven Wagner, Vice President of Programming for Hearst's Home Arts Network, spends his days bringing the company's magazines onto the World Wide Web. His evenings are shared with his wife, Maura McEvoy, a busy photographer, in their serenely chic 1,400-square-foot loft in Manhattan's SoHo district. If Steven has to bring work home, he retreats to a 25-by-15-foot office/guest room tucked into one comfortable corner of the loft.

Steven preferred not to completely close off his office from the rest of the loft, but he did want to ensure a sense of privacy—especially for when guests come to stay—so he turned to lighting designer Gaston Marticorena for help. Gaston created two scrims of white Lycra and stretched them across the space like sails, blocking off the desk, office area, and guest bed, yet allowing an unimpeded flow of light. He shaped the Lycra with a slight arc, to imbue each piece with a sculptural, organic feeling.

OPPOSITE: **A scrim of Lycra stretched on the diagonal separates the dining area from the home office. Another piece of Lycra tents the top for an enclosed feeling.**

ABOVE: **By positioning the office area in this corner of his loft, Steven can take advantage of the wonderful light spilling in from a bank of windows. The large laminate** desktop and additional **storage bins below provide adequate work surface. A brass bed and 1950's lamp add eclectic charm to the sophisticated setup.**

For storage, Steven converted an ordinary, off-the-shelf, ready-to-assemble Ikea cabinet into a mobile unit. Because he did not require two-way access to the shelves, he walled up the back of the cabinet with plywood. He then screwed heavy-duty trolley wheels to the bottom and affixed handles to the sides, so that the unit could be pushed around easily.

Steven's L-shaped desk, constructed from simple plastic laminate, stands on tubular steel legs that straddle a tall bookcase laid on its side. The sections in the bookcase are convenient for storing the everyday items he does not want to put in the roll-around unit. A comfortable curl-into chair provides the final touch to a space where both host and guests can be perfectly content.

LEFT: **Old country shutters from Maine help to deflect glare away from the computer screens, while webbing covers the unsightly radiators. Maura chose Mastex, a material commonly used for curtain backing, because it stretches. She wove** it into a web-like pattern and simply attached it with a staple gun to a plywood frame. Since the loft doesn't have much of a view, Steven and Maura provided one with vintage blueprints of the Chrysler Building. ABOVE AND OPPOSITE: **A** standard laminate shelf unit from Ikea can be wheeled into service to change the configuration of the office. Elegant bronze handles are fitted onto its side. Heavy-duty casters were purchased at a local hardware store for $10.00.

Brett Froomer, a commercial photographer, numbers Lexus, Jaguar, and Nikon among his major clients, and also keeps busy by shooting on location for *Condé Nast Traveler*. Susan Boyer, his wife and partner, runs their Manhattan studio and produces Brett's photo shoots. She is also mother to their small son Langdon Cole, age 2. To integrate the various aspects of their hectic lives, the Froomers decided to live and work out of the same space.

New York's Flatiron district, concentrated around the celebrated skyscraper of the same name, is home to many of the city's top photographers. Here the couple found the perfect location for their home/office: a 2,300-square-foot loft that was formerly a pin factory.

In their initial interview with architect Michael Dodson, Brett and Susan shared their concerns about combining a home life with their work. They were determined that a certain portion of the overall space be allotted for privacy. Bedrooms and bath were to be sacrosanct. The rest of the space was to be left open but designed in such a way as to mesh their domestic and professional lives. Brett and Susan wanted not only to meet with clients in their loft but also to entertain them there for dinner; linking their home office to an expansive living/dining area and

Rich blond wood encases the television in the living area, while an old pine dining table adds a reassuring touch. Diffused light filters through walls of Plexiglas onto a pair of cozy sofas from Shabby Chic.

open kitchen was crucial to the plan. Finally, of course, the loft had to appeal to the couple's aesthetic sensibilities.

Michael utilized two principal design elements—sculptural pieces of cabinetry and large, gridded, brushed-steel and fiberglass screens—to achieve the Froomers' goals. The cabinets, rendered in ash, animate the space with their unique organic forms, divide the office from the rest of the room without closing it off completely, and also hold storage. The screens act as partitions, too, but they also block an unsightly view while diffusing the natural light that falls into the space from a bank of floor-to-ceiling windows.

Michael situated the actual office area behind a low concrete-block wall right at the core of the loft. It is a compact space of approximately 170 square feet but can accommodate all the Froomers' needs due to its layout, which incorporates built-in along with freestanding file cabinets. A juxtaposition of boxed-in beams and thick columns set off the office. Conveniently, this strategy also created an entry hall that leads past the office into the open living area. Inconspicuous tracks of halogen bulbs flood both hallway and office with light.

OPPOSITE: **The lilting shapes of the twin sofas are echoed by the curve of a low wall that shields the home office from view. Zebra-print fabric enlivens an Alvar Aalto bentwood chair.**
ABOVE: **A cinder-block wall with slate countertop immediately distinguishes the work area from the rest of the loft.**

LEFT: **From the desk chair, the eye looks downward to a self-contained world of work, while an upward glance brings the warmth of the living area into view.**
ABOVE: **Brushed stainless steel stairs lead from the living room to a second small office area enclosed by Plexiglas panels.**

When one or more employees work with the owner in a home office, an environment must be creat-ed that protects the home owner's

personal space. At the same time, employees must be made to feel welcome and comfortable. Because space is frequently at a premium in

a home office, employer and employee often double up on equipment, such as the telephone or a computer; sharing a work surface

HOME-SUITE-HOME OFFICE

is also common. An inventive approach to working as a team often yields innovative results.

HOME-SUITE-HOME OFFICE

LOU ANN BAUER · SAN FRANCISCO

The first floor of an 1887 Victorian town house in the Haight-Ashbury district of San Francisco is the setting for the four-room suite of offices occupied by interior designer Lou Ann Bauer and her three full-time employees.

The floor plan, consisting of a large parlor in front, a casual living room and dining table in the middle, and a kitchen in the back, allowed Lou Ann to set up separate work spaces for herself and her staff. As the principal in her firm, she rightfully laid claim to the sunny front parlor for her own office. She then designated the old living room as the conference room. Large double doors connect it to the dining room, which now accommodates three workstations. Coffee and lunch are taken in the kitchen, which shares counter space with the fax machine, adding machine, and extra phone.

Lou Ann's signature sense of whimsy is omnipresent throughout her office. An avid collector of found objects and folk art, she also adores color, so a palette of more than a dozen luscious hues—including blueberry, chartreuse, tangerine and wheat—plays over the walls in every room.

Lou Ann consolidated all her design books and specifications manuals in one long free-form bookcase assembled from thick, rough-sawn boards balanced on boxes made of particleboard sprayed with Zolatone. Three old bowling balls sit on top of the stacked boxes—a humorous take on decorative finials.

LEFT: **One of San Francisco's many Victorian town houses.** RIGHT: **The only gray in sight in this color-filled environment is that of the matrix laminate conference room table. Chairs are birch plywood in several stains and shapes. Lou Ann placed shards of travertine marble in a mosaic pattern on the old fireplace. A computer workstation comes in handy during client meetings.**

LEFT: **A brushed stainless steel shoe rack finds its true calling as a wall filing unit.** RIGHT: **The staff work area demonstrates Lou Ann's daring way with color. She designed the pattern for the carpet and simply had the broadloom cut to fit, creating a one-of-a-kind floor. Waffled aluminum sheeting works as an inexpensive base for staff desks.**

ABOVE: **What to do with an old office chair from Knoll? Why, re-cover it in purple and chartreuse leather, of course. And don't forget the zigzag pattern. A collection of miniature chairs adorns the desktop.**

RIGHT: **A wall of shelving for books and catalogs was constructed by placing 2' x 21' planks on top of particleboard boxes that act as support columns. Bowling ball finials complete the assemblage.**

Lou Ann is particularly fond of taking everyday objects and turning them into something completely unexpected. A case in point is the vintage Knoll office chair she found in a used furniture store: she re-covered it in jazzy chartreuse and purple leather with a zigzag motif. Her own desk is a collage-like construction created by Ed Fickbolm, a San Francisco designer. Staff desks were made from waffled-aluminum sheeting normally used for barn siding, custom-cut to shroud the sides of standard-issue file cabinets. In describing her "anti-corporate aesthetic," this avid collector of found objects and folk art says, "My office reflects my personality. If our homes can be an expression of who we are, why can't our offices? Most people think we have to be so serious at work, but I completely disagree. The color, the objects, the art—they give me inspiration."

LEFT: **Lou Ann's decorating motto might well be "why paint a room one color when you can paint it two or three . . . or six?" Outsider art looks right at home next to San Francisco designer Keith Krumweide's tilted bookcase. Magazines hang on a floor-to-ceiling metal lattice. Lou Ann's desk is a quirky mix of painted wood and distressed iron made by Ed Fickbolm.**

TOP RIGHT: **Clients wait in a comfortable foyer. Chairs have been reupholstered with French cotton vinylized for easy cleaning. A jazzy aluminum vase holds fresh flowers.** RIGHT: **Kitchen cabinets of cobalt blue contain playful pottery, but the counter below is reserved for business: fax machine, telephone, postage meter, and scale are kept here.**

It's impossible to guess the location of Sarah Laird's office just by looking at it. The hectic, high-pressure business Sarah runs with her two best friends, Laura Foote and Key Whitehead, is in direct contrast to the quiet, peaceful Greenwich Village neighborhood in which it is situated. The trio represents photographers, fashion stylists and makeup artists for editorial work in magazines such as *Glamour* and *Self,* for advertising clients J. Crew and Clairol, and for MTV music videos.

All three of these energetic women hail from Mississippi. Sarah and Laura have been close friends since childhood, and Sarah's husband, Steve, had known Key for years. When it comes to hard work, the three partners share an uncommon synergy.

Six years ago, when Sarah and Steve had the first of their two children, Sarah began to think about starting her own company. Back then, as a new mother, she would sit on the bed, juggling the baby and the telephone, trying to book jobs for her one client. By the end of the year, she was representing 11 artists. Steve left his job at a law firm to handle all their financial and legal work. First Laura, then Key, joined the company, and the Lairds relocated both home and business to a 1,500-square-foot, 1850 carriage house.

TOP LEFT: **Sarah Laird calls this hidden corner of Greenwich Village home.** BOTTOM LEFT: **A balcony off the second-floor kitchen overlooks a quiet courtyard.** RIGHT: **The "machine table" in the foreground holds fax, printers, photocopier, and stereo. A rolling file cabinet tucked underneath houses a typewriter. The kitchen in the far left corner services both home and office, and an antique pine cupboard stores Sarah's sweaters.**

With original beamed ceilings still intact, rustic brick walls, and leaded stained-glass windows, the office feels more like a cottage in the country than the upper floor of a city carriage house. Steve designed the massive L-shaped pine desk, which sits on an Oriental carpet in the center of the space. This configuration allows for three individual workstations, while keeping the partners in close proximity so that they can collaborate when teamwork is necessary. A large lazy Susan in the center of the three work areas holds four Rolodexes and each artist's schedule. Key and Laura share a computer that moves back and forth between their desktops.

LEFT: **A lazy Susan gives the three women equal access to names, numbers, and client appointment books.**
RIGHT: **Both the desktop and the storage cabinet are made of pine.**

The "portfolio table" and the built-in cabinets storing photographers' portfolios, videos, and posters are also crafted of pine. Another large table, against the opposite wall, contains such basic office equipment as two printers, the fax and Xerox machines, and the stereo. Four file cabinets—including one on wheels —slide underneath.

LEFT: **A stained-glass window provides a stunning backdrop for an antique column. A floor lamp angled toward the ceiling casts warm reflected light.**
ABOVE: **Nestled in a small window alcove, a still life of books and photographs counters the chaos of the office.**
RIGHT: **The perfect place to review portfolios with a client is in the courtyard, graced with an old garden table.**

Having a home office is an excuse to go shopping for antiques, declares Doe Coover, a passionate collector of art, pottery, vintage metal toys, cookie jars, and quilts, whose daily life is consumed by her business as a literary agent. After spending many years as an editor in New York and, later, in Boston, she moved, as they say, from one side of the desk to the other and opened her own agency on the top floor of a rambling Victorian house in a Boston suburb. Moving her business into her home harmonized with her life as a wife and mother of two children.

Doe's first home office had been in a much smaller house, where she learned firsthand of the problems involved with working in a basement: humid summer weather made all the envelopes stick together, and whenever someone walked overhead, dust rained down on the desks. Her current home, by contrast, already had a fully renovated attic, with three rooms and a hallway—a perfect office space to grow into. Today, Doe shares the attic with a partner and an assistant, and there's adequate room for everyone.

During her renovation of the third floor, which included the addition of a new bathroom, the installation of built-in bookcases, and a mandatory paint job, Doe's love of collecting and eye for detail worked overtime. As a result, the wall of shelving

LEFT: **An antique wooden soap box holds Doe's outgoing mail.**
RIGHT: **The spareness of the oversized Mennonite table Doe uses as a desk contrasts with the whimsy of her collections. Lavender walls meet white ceiling to outline the shape of the garret office.**

LEFT: **The Rolodex is crucial to an agent's work, and Doe's takes pride-of-place next to her computer. Clients' books line the open shelves of a low wall. On top are Doe's collectibles, including old toy stoves. The television monitor allows her to view author videos from her desk.**
TOP RIGHT: **A tiny room carved out of the pitched section of the attic serves as a hideaway for private telephone conversations and manuscript reading.**
BOTTOM RIGHT: **A basket keeps Doe's numerous phone messages in one place. A side table is especially useful for its lower shelf, which can accommodate larger books and catalogs. On top, wire baskets keep projects neat and organized.**

devoted to clients' books also showcases some of her treasured flea-market finds. Office supplies are kept in a pine cabinet originally used to hang church vestments. Doe discovered her desk—an expansive antique farm table from Indiana—at a Mennonite furniture store. Since it had no drawers, she set another table, made of recycled pine, nearby. On top sit five wire baskets that are used to organize contracts and other pending works, keeping her desk clear of paper.

Working at home offers Doe the added advantage

ABOVE: **Rather than keep her large photocopier in the office, Doe relegated it to the landing, where her assistants can use it for long periods of time without disturbing her.**

RIGHT: **A selection of Doe's cookie jar collection is displayed on top of an old church vestment cabinet. Inside are office supplies. The Techline storage towers have adjustable shelves perfect for stacking manuscripts.**

of being within earshot of her children when they come home from school. Plus, the kids enjoy having office supplies at their disposal. When Doe is out of town, the fax machine provides a special way for the family to stay in touch. Her son even faxed her his report card once!

The hills of Beverly Glen Canyon captivated Gregg Homer many years ago. He was 17 when he and his father first moved here, into a small bungalow-style home. Upon graduating from law school, Gregg purchased the house from his father.

Since then he has married and now has four children of his own.

LEFT: **Gregg's Los Angeles home has one feature no downtown skyscraper could hope to match—an indoor-outdoor office. A wisteria-covered pergola shelters the slate-topped conference table.** RIGHT: **The pergola perches above the carport.**

After 16 years spent working in large law firms, Gregg, an entertainment lawyer, decided to move his practice to his home. He retained Tim Guetzlaff from Design Partnership to design an addition to the house, with the ground level devoted to rooms for his children and the upper floor reserved for his business. The office Tim designed shares the front entrance to the house, but a separate stairway immediately off the main hall leads up to Gregg's quarters. The reception area at the top of the stairs is ample enough to accommodate Gregg's secretary, a wall of storage, and a small bathroom. Double doors of sandblasted glass lead to his private office. Because the room is unusually long and narrow—21-by-13 feet—Tim designed built-in cabinets and a 14-foot-long desk/counter with open storage above to hug two walls.

All were crafted of pale blond maple. On this expansive work surface Gregg can stack papers and files from various projects he might be working on simultaneously.

Tim's unique design for computer storage pays homage to an old rolltop desk. In his contemporary version, tambour doors travel laterally across a track to hide or reveal the computer.

The corner of the room by the windows was reserved for a curvilinear update of a 1950's banquette, upholstered in luxurious cotton bouclé. The coffee table, designed by Pascal Mourgue, moves about on wheels.

A second-floor patio above the carport became an outdoor conference room. Wide glass doors lead from behind Gregg's desk out to a pyramid-shaped redwood pergola, which shelters a slate-topped conference table equipped with phone jacks and electrical outlets.

ABOVE: **In the casual atmosphere of his home office, Gregg can meet with his secretary and visit with his baby daughter Sophia at the same time.** LEFT: **A decorative wrought- iron railing with subtle red accents was added to the private stairway leading to the office. Additional storage was carved out of the space underneath.** RIGHT: **Cream-colored walls blend well with the neutral tones of a gracefully curved banquette. The coffee table is by Pascal Mourgue.**

LEFT: **The shape and structure of custom-built maplewood cabinets and desk balance the asymmetrical proportions of the office. The Madison swivel chair is by Donghia. Double glass doors let the outside in.** TOP RIGHT: **The maplewood tambour doors were custom-designed to slide sideways on tracks. Identical cubes of open shelves extend the length of the desk.** RIGHT: **Tambour doors slide open to reveal the computer monitor.**

Randy Whitehead's Potrero Hill home. RIGHT: **African masks and framed photographs make the hall between home and office a pleasant passageway.** OPPOSITE: **A 15-foot-long laminate countertop is big enough for three workstations. From underneath, file cabinets on wheels can be moved about for added flexibilty. The computer keyboard is ergonomically designed for maximum comfort and use.**

When Randy Whitehead purchased a row house in the Potrero Hill section of San Francisco, he knew exactly where to locate the home office for his new lighting design company, Lightsource: in the garage. This 15'-by-10', 150-square-foot space, although long and narrow, appealed to him because it could be entered through a hallway separate from the rest of the house. In addition, it had already been converted into a room with an oversized window that faced the street.

Randy devoted one entire long wall of the room to workstations for himself and his two assistants. Instead of custom-designing storage, he installed a series of standard-issue, laminate-covered, 14-inch-deep base cabinets above the work surface. He then hinged their toekicks to provide extra storage for small items.

White laminate also covers the room-length countertop, which, at 30 inches, is deeper than average, allowing books and other necessities to be stored behind the computers. Files and cabinets for office supplies roll out on casters from underneath.

To avoid wasting space, Randy recessed an old fold-down legal file into the wall and contrived a tall, narrow cabinet filled with PVC tubes to hold rolled-up drawings. The conference table is a simple "mouse

ear" of faux-granite laminate extending from the counter, which holds the fax and a drafting board.

As a lighting designer, Randy was especially aware of the need to light the space well. Fluorescent tubing above the wall cabinets deflects light to the ceiling and casts a warm, ambient glow; a valance screens similar tubing below to light the work surface. Glass bricks inserted into a jog in the wall at the far end of the room draw light from the large window into the adjoining hall.

LEFT: **PVC tubing stores cumbersome lighting plans inside a 6'-x-1' column. As a lighting designer, Randy enjoys the translucent quality of glass blocks. Here he has covered their edges with tile and topped them off with three cast concrete spheres that echo his company logo.** TOP RIGHT: **The old style fold-down file cabinet was a** $25.00 **flea market find. It was repainted at an auto body shop and recessed into the wall to save space.** BOTTOM RIGHT: **Because they are deeper than standard wall units, base cabinets were mounted above the desk area. The toekick space was hinged to provide additional storage. A blue laminate valance conceals task lighting.**

A column table lamp echoes the classical lines of the John Hancock Tower. OPPOSITE: The serpentine dining table rests on painted black sontubes (dense cardboard concrete molds). Next to the Noguchi lamp, a life-size interior photograph from the 1930s extends the room in trompe l'oeil fashion.

John Maienza lives in the quintessential Chicago high-rise. With its corner position on the 48th floor and an expanse of wraparound windows, his two-bedroom apartment offers him something a traditional home office might not—convenience coupled with spectacular views of downtown Chicago and Lake Michigan.

After working for several architectural and design firms in New York City, John relocated to Chicago to establish his own practice. Instead of taking a separate office, he decided to convert his 15'-by-33', 500-square-foot living room into an office for himself and a full-time assistant. A collection of furniture from the 1950s dictated the basic design. John then created additional pieces to complement what he already owned. For example, a kidney-shaped conference/work table made of birch plywood and stained a honey-brown echoes a favorite '50s silhouette. He can convert it into a dining table for guests simply by pulling up a pair of George Nelson chairs from 1952. A similarly curvy workstation for his assistant was designed with a raised front panel that conceals day-to-day clutter. Items that require John's immediate attention are placed on a small writing ledge at the top of the panel.

LEFT: **The assistant's desk was designed to complement the conference table.** BELOW: **A collection of glass vases from the 1960s adds a splash of color and style to an otherwise utilitarian file cabinet.** OPPOSITE: **The curved front panel of the assistant's desk conceals the clutter of work in progress, while the top ledge serves as an additional writing surface.**

John's personal work area is tucked into the corner of the L-shaped room, giving him an unobstructed view of his two favorite buildings in Chicago, the John Hancock Tower and the Palmolive Building. Two black file cabinets support a black laminate desktop. Because they are not used for storage, John turned them to fit the space.

John's affection for 20th-century American design classics is not limited to the 1950s. His home office also features a '40s Moderne black Naugahyde and chrome love seat and a Bertoia chair dating from the '60s. In this eclectic mix, a tall Noguchi lamp stands as a timeless piece of sculpture.

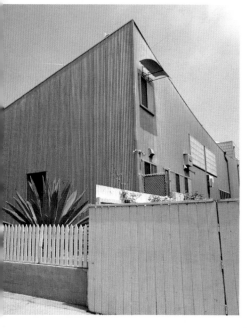

Dennis Hopper's home in Venice, California. RIGHT: **When at home, Hopper's base of operations is a large dining table set in the middle of his open-plan house. A skylight punctuates the ceiling while metal latticework gleams below it.**

A look behind the scenes at the home of actor Dennis Hopper reveals a domestic environment as unique as its owner. The celebrated actor, whose brilliant work in such well known films as *Easy Rider* (1969), *Apocalypse Now* (1979), *Blue Velvet* (1986), and *Speed* (1994) has captivated audiences for three decades, inhabits an atypical California home. In keeping with his idiosyncratic nature, Hopper chose to live in one of the toughest neighborhoods of Venice, California— no swimming pools or manicured gardens here. Clad in corrugated steel, his house, designed by architect Brian Murphy, stands out from its surroundings.

Hopper does not only work on location or in film studios; he also runs his own company, Alta Light Productions, from his home. His vice president, Robin Berg, is responsible for overseeing the scheduling of film work and related events, and coordinates how scripts and new material reach him. In addition to acting, Hopper is a prolific photographer and painter whose work has been shown in Japan and Prague, so Robin also organizes his exhibitions and assists with the selection of images for a show.

BELOW: **A wedge of glass blocks adds a gentle curve to an otherwise angular room.**
RIGHT: **Robin's domain is entered from the second level. An oak table serves as the desk, and various antique cabinets hold the fax machine and books.**

ABOVE: **An assemblage of tro-phies awarded to Hopper for his film work is displayed on a tabletop.** RIGHT: **One of Hopper's early works of pho-tography, a 12-panel photo silk screen, hangs opposite from Robin's desk. The metal café table and chairs are dwarfed by its scale.**

Hopper took an active role in the design of his home, especially its interiors, which have an open, loft-like feeling to showcase his impressive collection of 20th-century art. When at home, he prefers to sit at a large dining table where he can handle phone work, read scripts, and spread out contact sheets and photographs. The table, imported from Europe, came out of a hacienda he once owned in Taos, New Mex-ico. Although the table appears commanding within the context of the work space, the accompanying art, by contemporary artists and friends Kenny Scharf, David Salle, and Julian Schnabel, makes an even more dramatic statement.

Robin's office is reached by a wood and steel ramp off the living room. The ramp leads to a freestanding, double-height space in a building designed by archi-tect Frank Gehry. Sun-filled, with huge windows, the office appears casual and unpretentious. Here, Hopper's own artwork figures prominently in the decor: a 12-panel, photo silk screen he completed in 1967 fills one wall; on another, black-and-white photographs cap-ture faces from the '60s. Movie posters, awards, and memorabilia add to the visual mix.

Sharing a home office with a partner or spouse is an exercise in harmony. Many CHAPTER 5 couples who have established separate careers outside the home find that they must adapt to each other and develop new ways of working, both independently and as a team. Most importantly, the design

of a double work space must respond to personal needs:

one couple might kibbitz

across an updated partners

desk, while another might

realize that their individual work habits

require separate work **TEAM PLAYERS**

zones—even if they still share some of

the primary office equip-

ment, such as a printer,

a fax, or a copy machine.

CHAPTER 5

TEAM PLAYERS

JUDY & SID ZUBER · PHOENIX

The shadow-filled passageway and long interior ramp that lead into the home and office of Sidney and Judy Zuber feel as exotic and enigmatic as the Arizona desert surrounding the house. Designed by renowned Southwest architect Antoine Predock, whose work is often described as "mystical and intuitive," the Zuber house is carved into a mountain. To make the home office into a meditative "study cave," Predock wedged it, too, into the earth. Partially burying and berming home and office also keeps temperatures, which can rise into the 100s, under control.

Both husband and wife maintain offices outside their home—Judy heads a public-relations firm and Sid is a pathologist—but both needed a place to work in the evenings and on weekends, should the occasion arise.

The 450-square-foot office is positioned next to a semi-enclosed, terraced courtyard filled with pools of water—a commodity that in the desert is considered not only precious but sacred. When the large windowpanes along the courtyard-facing office wall are slid open, the sound of water rushing over the rim of the upper pool fills the room. The waterfall, which runs continuously, is another one of Predock's ploys to help cool the office naturally; recirculating water cools adjacent surfaces by evaporation.

ABOVE: **In the entryway, architect Antoine Predock made the most of the desert's natural design motif—light. The interplay of sun and shadow create a constantly changing pattern on the floor and walls.** RIGHT: **The soothing sound of spilling water echoes throughout a courtyard between the office and the main house.**

LEFT: **Along the walls of the hallway leading to the home office, photographs and objects placed on lighted glass shelves act as magnets, drawing visitors into the space.** ABOVE: **The combination of painted white** walls and clean maplewood creates a neutral decor perfect for examining and evaluating artworks. While the rug looks like pure Southwest Indian, the design is actually by 1920s Viennese master Josef Hoffmann.

As serious collectors, Judy and Sid wanted their office to function also as a place to research and read about art. They asked Predock to keep the backdrop neutral so that they could contemplate pottery, sculpture, photography, or paintings within the context of the room.

Predock suggested pale maple for the cabinets and desk. The cabinets, simple and symmetrical in their design and configuration, support a room-length desktop, which the Zubers share. A pair of classic Knoll desk chairs pull in to their individual workstations, and open shelves run above. The carpet, a Josef Hoffmann design from the 1920s, takes on new meaning in this setting, its simple geometry conveying a modern minimalism.

OPPOSITE: **Black canvas along the 22-foot-long desk creates an expansive bulletin board for art notices, favorite images, and memos. Cabinets below the desktop are used for storage.** LEFT: **Judy personalized her space with a collection of crystal and silver inkwells given to her by her father.**

JAMES & DEBORAH BREMNER • LOS ANGELES

For Deborah and James Bremner, working at home is a family experience. Both are real-estate agents affiliated with a busy Brentwood office, but they prefer the cozy, well-appointed, 15'-by-18', 170-square-foot office adjoining their dining room. Working from home allows them to spend considerably more time with their three children, one of which is a new baby. Their older children take advantage of the office, too: 12-year-old Ben often pulls up a chair to the glass-topped end of the desk to do his homework, and Jennifer, 16, frequently comes in to access the Internet.

To plan one office that would efficiently accommodate two people, Deborah and James turned to Nick Berman, a Los Angeles furniture and interior designer. Because the room is fairly compact, Nick concentrated all storage and work space in one integral unit that includes cabinets, shelves, and work surfaces for both Bremners.

LEFT: **The facade of the Bremners' house in Brentwood reveals little about the inside: its laconic, almost temple-like quality recalls similar houses Frank Lloyd Wright designed in Los Angeles earlier this century.**
RIGHT: **With a shared partners desk and two of everything, symmetry prevails. A disc of sandblasted glass at the end of the desk functions as an extra work space or a conference table. The Sapper Executive desk chairs are from Knoll.**

LEFT: **One benefit of working from home: more family time. Deborah's new baby enjoys playing on the desktop.**
BELOW: **"Junior partner" Ben, the Bremners' 12-year-old son, sometimes pulls up a chair to do his homework at the end of the desk.** RIGHT: **The center storage strip houses television, stereo, modem, and computer monitor. It is flanked by two 8-foot-high storage cabinets with smoky green glass doors.**

The commodious desk—the focal point of the entire setup—is based on a traditional partners desk. Nick designed the piece, which he affectionately describes as a "buddy desk," to encourage interaction between husband and wife when they collaborate on projects. Each separate work space is tailored to its occupant's personal work habits. Bracing the desk is a tall three-bay cabinet flanked by open shelving and twin base cabinets that stretch the full width of the room.

The couple's office styles are, indeed, different. Deborah is very organized and prefers to work on one thing at a time; she also likes the portability of a laptop computer. James, on the other hand, tends to have

lots of papers around, and he chooses to work with the large desktop computer tucked into one niche of the wall system. As he can handle more clutter than can his wife, they agreed to cover two of the cabinet's bays with green glass doors that visually muffle whatever James might decide to stack on the shelves.

The desk, 7 by 10 feet long, is made of the same cherrywood as the tall, desk-width cabinet unit. Twin teal-colored leather "blotters" are sunk into the desktop. The cherry trim that sets them off expands to what Nick calls the "pool"—a round inset of sandblasted glass that does double duty as a conference table.

Lighting recessed into the ceiling frees the desk of tabletop fixtures. Daylight streams in through a bank of 10-foot-high windows; a linen shade that raises from the bottom adds a sense of privacy while allowing ample light to fill the room.

OPPOSITE: **Eight-foot-tall double doors of sandblasted glass separate the home office from the family's dining room.** TOP: **A keyboard tray slides under the desktop and the monitor swivels so that Deborah and James (and visiting clients) can view the screen together.** BOTTOM: **"Floating" file cabinets on casters can be easily moved around the room. James keeps his next to the reading chair; Deborah prefers hers alongside her desk.**

In 1973, when Barbara and Wayne King moved into their house in Ipswich, Massachusetts, they would never have guessed that one day they would both work at home. Today, Wayne, a structural engineer, and Barbara, a potter, operate businesses from a turn-of-the-century, 3,000-square-foot barn that adjoins the house via a breezeway.

After teaching art for many years, Barbara quit her job to devote herself full time to making pottery and running the Ocmulgee Pottery gallery, which now occupies the ground floor of the barn. After 21 years at a large architectural/engineering firm in Cambridge, Wayne foresaw that he would be laid off. In response, he started his own business.

When Wayne decided to situate his office in the barn, division of the space was not an issue. Even though Barbara had already established her studio in the basement, which had originally housed horse and cow stalls, and the gallery took up the ground floor, that still left plenty of room—more than 900 square feet, in fact. Wayne turned the 12'-by-20' second floor over to his drafting table and work area. The third floor, a compact 15'-by-20' former hayloft, is now a conference room.

Each morning, the Kings share a short walk to work through the breezeway. Also shared are the fax, pho-

Wayne's laminate desktop is raised slightly above the bookcase, giving it an architectural look and also providing a place to store small items. Barbara's section of the office is in the far corner. A ledge under the eaves becomes a decorative niche.

tocopy machines, computer printer—and coffee break. The two maintain separate phone lines and computers; Barbara's sits in the corner of Wayne's office, where she has set up a workstation to tackle the weekly paperwork connected with the gallery. When necessary, she can connect her laptop to the printer.

Wayne substantially cut costs on the renovation of the upper floors by doing the work on the office himself. In a large structure such as a barn, adequate lighting is a major consideration. Up under the eaves, in the conference room, Wayne cleverly turned a set of barn windows on its side to function "like a shoji screen" across an interior wall. The windows ricochet light from skylights set into the steeply pitched roof to the room below. A second set of interior windows, painted bright turquoise, glances from Barbara's workstation into the open-eaved stairwell leading up from the gallery.

To give himself a sufficient work surface and accessible storage, Wayne set up a U-shaped configuration incorporating an adjustable drafting table and stable desktop, file cabinets, and shelving in one corner of the remodeled room. He notched Barbara's workstation into a corner directly across from his own, right next to the stairway. Gray industrial carpeting and pale yellow walls trimmed in oak and accented with turquoise unify all areas.

OPPOSITE: **The compactness of Wayne's work area is evident when seen from the conference room window above. His desk, drafting table, and bookshelf create a convenient, efficient, U-shaped work space. The printer rests on an old sewing machine table the couple unearthed in the attic.**
ABOVE: **A portable white plastic trolley holds Barbara's files. Her computer is housed in a wooden ergonomic console with a slide-out drawer for the keyboard.**

LEFT: **The conference room is on the top floor, under the pitched roof of the barn's former hayloft. The sofa doubles as a guest bed. To the right, windows overlooking Wayne's office on the second floor have been fitted sideways to open horizontally.** TOP RIGHT: **From the doorway, the initial view of the main office space shows not a desk but an antique oak dining table. It serves as an extra work surface or a place to have lunch. Pottery lines the ledge by the stairs leading up from the gallery.** BOTTOM RIGHT: **The hallway houses the large blueprint machine. Shuttered closet doors along the wall conceal office supplies.**

In the high elevations of the Sonoran Desert south of Tucson, Arizona, the landscape unfolds to reveal rolling grasslands and windswept, mesquite-studded hills. Here, in Sonoita, not only the incredible beauty but also the accessibility of a major airport were determining factors in building a house with two home offices for a private investor and his

The silhouette of the traditional adobe house stands out against the mesquite-covered landscape. RIGHT: **His office: A bold kilim from Afghanistan placed on the pigmented and polished concrete floor mixes perfectly with the Southwest feel of the room.**

wife, an investment banker with offices in New York and San Francisco.

From November to April, the couple lives in their desert house. As a concession to this lifestyle, the wife travels constantly—as much as four days a week. Describing the serenity she finds in this "magical escape," she remarks upon how the desert eases the stress of her otherwise hectic schedule.

When planning their individual work spaces, the couple consulted Elaine Paul from Arroyo Design. The designer first suggested a partners desk for the two, but, because their work styles differ quite radically,

TOP: **His office keeps "high tech" to a minimum—but there is a fax that rests on a file cabinet made of mesquite to match the desk.** BOTTOM: **Weathered skulls bleached bone-white by the desert sun make unusual paperweights.** OPPOSITE: **His place in the sun: when closed, shutters made from saguaro cactus ribs still let in dappled light. The tall Alderwood bookshelves are edged with a simple molding, as is the desk.**

both husband and wife were set on having two separate offices. He confesses to being strictly a "telephone and yellow pad" person who does not require a computer; she, by contrast, uses a laptop, which connects by modem to her office in New York City. They share a fax machine. This stands on a file cabinet in his office to provide access to documents he requests through the library of a nearby university. In addition to organizing the interiors, Elaine designed and manufactured custom furniture for both offices. Most of the pieces are crafted of mesquite wood. In his 192-square-foot office, a traditional desk sits on a contemporary 16-foot rug by one window, with the matching file cabinet and fax alongside. Shutters fabricated of saguaro cactus ribs block the intense desert sun. A comfortable sofa and lounge chair offer cozy spots to catch up on papers and reading.

LEFT: **Brass hardware gives an old-fashioned feel to the richly oiled mesquite desk. A copper lamp and a magnifying glass on a brass stand add to the gleam. The detailing on the mesquite and ironwood chair by Arroyo**

Design is reminiscent of the American Arts and Crafts style.
ABOVE: **Her lighter touch: a graceful Queen Anne writing desk is angled to face the spectacular desert view. The piece, by Arroyo Design,**

is also made of mesquite. Shell-pattern molding (a motif borrowed from Spanish missions in the Southwest) turns a small window into a scalloped niche. The daybed is of cherrywood.

A delicate Queen Anne writing desk occupies one corner of her 12'-by-14', 168-square-foot office, which is located just across the hall from her husband's. From this vantage point, she can bask in the desert view from a pair of windows situated above a long settee. The floor is covered with a non-distracting, neutral-toned sisal rug upon which rests a collection of Apache water baskets. Woven rattan files, found at a shop in downtown New York, store papers.

LEFT: **From his to hers: the two rooms are visible from either side of a tiled hallway.** RIGHT: **Woven rattan boxes are large enough to hold legal-size documents.**

OPPOSITE: **The art above her desk parallels the view from the windows. A collection of Apache water baskets sits upon the simple sisal rug, and assorted colorful pillows adorn the settee.**

The porch and entrance to Kate's home office are just a few steps from where Eric works. RIGHT: Eric is able to wander between his work space and Kate's. Best of all, he gets to play with baby daughter Olivia.

A small, freestanding building for her, the lower level of their Sausalito home for him: that's how Kate McIntyre and husband Eric Christensen work in their respective offices. Kate is president and co-owner of Ironies, a furniture company that specializes in iron furniture and cast stone. Eric is a "thematic designer" who worked with filmmaker George Lucas on special effects and on models for movie sets until he decided to break away and establish a business of his own. Now he is responsible for the look of Fry's electronic stores, a large West Coast retailer whose interiors resemble Alice's Wonderland or ancient Egypt.

Kate had been working in Oakland at Ironies' production studio and corporate offices, but after she gave birth to daughter Olivia, she followed Eric's lead and began to plan a home office of her own. With fax, phone, and modem, she knew that communication with her corporate office would be easy and would leave her plenty of time to tend to her baby. She adopted a small building—which once housed the printing press for the first Marin newspaper in Sausalito—as her home base and moved it next to the house, where a balustraded outside deck links it to Eric's office.

Kate's office, which measures 300 square feet, was designed with simplicitiy in mind. A built-in desk/ counter with overhead cabinets for storage occupies one corner of the mint-green room. The height of the work surface—and of a platform bed—was determined by an existing, exposed concrete foundation wall. Kate sheathed the concrete with beaded board. She then applied a product she designs, "Pietra Dura" stone, into a colorful, seashell-patterned desktop, which "T's" around an existing structural column. In the raised bed area, crisp white bed linens and a plump duvet against one of her Ironies headboards create a restful place for relaxing—or a private space for overnight guests. A drafting table situated in front of the oversized window next to the bed affords her ample natural light and a view of the trees.

OPPOSITE: **Kate works at a counter composed of Pietra Dura, the stone product she designs. White cabinets and cool mint-green walls give a serene feeling to the space. The chandelier resting on the floor is a prototype of one of her creations, and the stool is from Pottery Barn.**

TOP: **A bench of Kate's design bestows a romantic air to one corner of her office. Eric's work space is visible across the porch deck.** BOTTOM: **The guest bed is tucked away on a cozy platform along one wall. An Ironies base originally used for a dining table now supports the drafting table.**

Eric's glass-enclosed, 10'-by-25', 250-square-foot office was built from a pre-existing porch. Casement windows set at chair rail height line two sides of the room. His drafting table, like Kate's, tucks into the windowed corner, so he too can look at the trees. An antique mission-style table against the wall directly behind it holds Eric's computer, allowing him to swivel his chair, pull a lever, and drop down from drafting table to desk height. Eric also prefers clutter-free work surfaces, so books, catalogs, and papers are stored on shelves in an adjoining hallway built to function as a small library.

Perhaps the perfect office situation is one in which you can be at home and away from it at the same time. If your office is but a few steps from the house, you can walk to work in a matter of minutes and hit the coffee machine for a second cup without too much effort.

Working in an outbuilding offers a unique sense of freedom. Whether it opens onto a courtyard, is carved out of a back-yard, or stands alone BRANCHING OUT on a hillside, each office is treasured by its owner as a sanctuary. Tranquil and inviting, these "worlds apart" in-crease productivity and enhance daily life.

BRANCHING OUT

DAVID LINDSEY · AUSTIN · TX

The home office of popular mystery writer David Lindsey (*Requiem for a Glass Heart*; *Mercy*) is a temple to the written word. Perched on a bluff overlooking rolling hills of craggy limestone escarpments dotted with oaks and cedars, its site, near Austin, Texas, is the spot where David had dreamed of building his office for many years.

When first pondering a design, David turned to his vast collection of books for ideas. Through his research, he learned that concrete was used in early construction, particularly in ancient Roman architecture. Inspired by this bit of history, he and his architect, Alfred Godfrey, determined that the cast-in-place arches supporting the roof in the new structure would be concrete. The floors were also to be made of this material.

There's a sense of mystery in the air from the moment one enters the building through a small door. Although the space is quite large (1,500 square feet) and open, it feels intimate and quiet—almost ecclesiastical— partly because it was conceived as a library as well as an office. Like the finest university library, David's office is grandly scaled, with cherrywood bookcases of various heights encircling the room. Although his present collection numbers over 4,000 volumes, David requested extra shelving to anticipate future acquisitions.

LEFT AND BELOW: **Mystery writer David Lindsey's free-standing office looks like a centuries-old church. A Romanesque arch marks the entrance.** RIGHT: **Delicately detailed concrete trusses support the arched ceiling while the scored patterns in the floor suggest a medieval crypt below.**

Another feature of the library, the fireplace, provides a gathering point for a cozy seating group where David can entertain or read. Personal items—Oaxacan pottery, cigar boxes, tobacco tins, and inkwells—adorn a low shelf in front of the windows. Combining arched panes and casements, these windows play a prominent role in the space: they filter golden light from the west and their dramatic views inspire David as he crafts one of his mysteries.

OPPOSITE: **Tall windows are topped with large arched fan lights for maximum sunlight. Lantern-like lamps illuminate the library in the evening.** BELOW: **David reviews his manuscripts in a cozy spot by the fireplace.**

The huge room features three desks. One is a classically detailed, 18th-century pedestal desk, where the telephone sits. Another, smaller piece, also dating from the 18th century, holds the computer. The third, a table that David uses as his main workstation, was crafted by a local artisan, Mark Landers. All three desks are made of mahogany.

LEFT: **David's collections of cigar boxes and inkwells are spread out along the window ledge.** ABOVE: **Every bookshelf doesn't have to be filled to the gills. In the empty spaces, David strategically displays Guatemalan pottery and Mexican woodcuts. The recessed drawer pulls,** finely detailed with a beaded edge in cast bronze, were found 12 years ago in a San Antonio antique shop. OPPOSITE: **David's office features three mahogany desks. The computer and writing tables both date from the 18th century. The third desk was created by a local artisan.**

The desire for space, light, and flexibility is common among those who work at home; to this list Steven Raichlen would add mobility. His decision to relocate from Boston to Miami to marry his wife, Barbara, fulfilled all his wishes. As a chef, food writer, and well-known cookbook author (*Miami Spice*; *The Caribbean Pantry Cookbook*), Steven had long wanted to work in a place congruent with his subject matter.

In Florida, houses often come with small cottages, or "dependencies," behind them—a pleasant surprise for Steven. Between the main house and the outbuilding he could indulge his penchant for moving about with his laptop as inspiration strikes. The location he and Barbara found also allows him to bike to a nearby park to write whenever he feels like it.

The 25'-by-20', 500-square-foot cottage, originally a garage, had previously been partially renovated, so converting it into a home office required few structural changes. New French doors and windows, matching those in the main house, flood the formerly dark room with light. To enhance the effect, Steven revitalized the inexpensive paneling and plasterboard ceiling inherited from the former owners with a

Cookbook author Steven Raichlen converted the garage behind his home in Miami into an office. With its well-stocked shelves, the building could be mistaken for a country bookstore.
OPPOSITE: **The desk, made of wood counters resting on black file cabinets, wraps around two walls of windows in an L-shaped configuration that allows Steven to enjoy the outdoors at all times.**

glowing coat of fresh white paint. He then filled one entire wall of the office with several hundred feet of bookshelves to organize his thousands of cookbooks and a treasured collection of French novels.

Steven likes to spread out as many as 10 projects at a time over a broad surface. The inspiration for his desks—butcher-block counters straddling file cabinets—derived from his student days. Many of the file cabinets he'd had for years; others were picked up at garage sales. As assembled, the desks wrap one corner of the room, with Steven's work area running alongside the windows. A trestle table, with phone, juts out near one of the doors.

Fortunately for Steven, the cottage was large enough to incorporate not only an old rolltop but also a couch, which offers him an alternative place to sit with his laptop on rainy days, when he can't take his work

outside. The couch, modeled after a Craftsman settee by Arts and Crafts proponent Gustav Stickley, was made for him in a barter arrangement in which Steven traded a year's worth of cooking classes for the piece.

LEFT: **For Steven, who likes to roam around when he writes, the laptop computer is the perfect invention; plain old-fashioned notebooks also come in handy. The bottles contain ingredients from his recipe for homemade pineapple rum.** ABOVE TOP: **The shady courtyard in front of the office is one of Steven's favorite spots for writing.** ABOVE: **Since Steven sells his line of specially** prepared spices directly from his office, he needs a proper mail room. A scale, packing and postage supplies, and a copy machine are all kept in apple-pie order. OPPOSITE: **Windows galore and a clean white interior combine to create the ultimate writer's retreat. The solidity of an entire wall of books contrasts with the airy tropical ease of the cottage.**

Meg Strattner enjoys new challenges. When she and Peter, her husband (and co-owner of the Asher Benjamin studio, where they design Shaker-inspired furniture), were propelled into parenthood by their adoption of two children from Russia, it didn't take her long to realize that her career would have to shift to part-time status.

A guest cottage on the Strattners' property was the perfect spot to convert into a home office. With windows on all sides and a high, pitched ceiling, the cottage boasted wonderful light and an open, airy atmosphere. A kitchenette was already in place, as was a small bathroom, so no mechanical or structural updates were required.

Meg had been involved with the design of the Herman Miller TD collection, a line of cherrywood office furniture scaled for residential use, and had tested the prototype in her studio. When she decided to relocate to the cottage, she brought the whole system home.

The TD desk, constructed as an angled ell, culminates in a quarter-round drop leaf, which flips up to create an extra work surface. Meg set it up to face both the windows and the door—a perfect spot for checking

ABOVE: **A guest cottage on the Strattners' property was converted into a home office.** OPPOSITE: **Designing Shaker-style furniture is Meg's professional calling and personal passion. No 17th-century craftsman could have dreamed of a swiveling Windsor chair on casters—but Meg realized it was the perfect way to update this much-loved classic. The office suite is from the Herman Miller TD collection.**

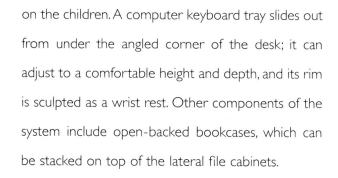

on the children. A computer keyboard tray slides out from under the angled corner of the desk; it can adjust to a comfortable height and depth, and its rim is sculpted as a wrist rest. Other components of the system include open-backed bookcases, which can be stacked on top of the lateral file cabinets.

Meg opted to push her tallest TD cabinet into a closet, allowing her to hide a mini-refrigerator on one of the shelves. The remainder of the unit stores supplies she doesn't need at her fingertips. The rest of the space is furnished like a family room—which it can become at a moment's notice.

OPPOSITE TOP LEFT: **The solid cherrywood desk includes a ledge that props up to act as an easel and a graceful hinged drop leaf that extends the work surface.** OPPOSITE BOTTOM LEFT: **Large file drawers hold both letter- and legal-sized documents.** OPPOSITE BOTTOM RIGHT: **Meg stacks supplies in the TD collection vertical storage cabinet she tucked into an unobtrusive alcove. It holds files, paper, stationery, and a mini-fridge that features artwork by her son Vladimir.** TOP RIGHT: **A New England peaked roof fitted with glass becomes a cheerful source of sunlight. The office doubles as a family gathering spot, complete with piano.** RIGHT: **After school the children share a moment with Meg and Peter. In anticipation of a new baby, the office has been equipped with a crib!**

The "hill country" surrounding Austin, Texas, is picturesque, peaceful, and surprisingly reminiscent of both Tuscany and rural Mexico. In fact, the city's architecture often shows influences from each region, and Sherry Smith's home office is no exception. Housed in a 26-foot-high, freestanding tower, the office was designed to complement the topography and to recall the foursquare towers so prevalent in northern Italy.

After many years at a local advertising agency, Sherry decided to strike out on her own and start a marketing company specializing in public relations and copywriting services. She did not, however, want to run the business out of her house but rather out of a separate office—a place where she could "go to work."

Once Sherry and her architects, Steinbomer and Associates, determined that the office should be situated in a tower, Sherry asked that its Tuscan demeanor be spiked with "a Mexican twist." As a result, the two-story tower's limestone exterior is accented with cobalt-blue doors and window trim.

ABOVE: **Welcome to Tuscany, Texas. Or at least to a slice of timeless Tuscan architecture with a contemporary touch— the asymmetrical triangle placed around the cobalt blue door.** LEFT: **The office as seen from the exercise room above.** BELOW: **Sherry relaxes on rustic limestone steps that make the building look as though it had been standing there for ages.**

Sherry's cool, gray-walled office occupies the lower of the tower's 14-square-foot levels; the upper floor is given over to an exercise room. The perimeter of this second story is punctuated by twelve 2-foot-square windows.

Sherry's desktop, which runs the full length of a wall dominated by a triple-bay window, consists of a generous expanse of black laminate trimmed in red. A pair of lateral files fits under one end of the desk; others line up along a perpendicular wall. Additional storage is provided by wire roll-around baskets and by Metro shelving.

For client meetings, Sherry uses a small round table made of metal and sandblasted glass from a local design store, and metal stacking chairs from Germany. Aware of the importance of ergonomics, she splurged on her desk chair, a bright red, high-back Equa chair from Herman Miller.

TOP LEFT: **A 14-foot-long expanse of black laminate trimmed in bright red forms the desk. The practical luxury of two chairs—one ergonomic office chair from Herman Miller (see page 190), the other in cool red leather from the Spiegel Catalogue—doubles the efficiency of the space. Halogen track lighting is combined with two task lights placed on either end of the** desk. **Rolling wire baskets are elegant, efficient, and inexpensive.** LEFT: **A woven Indonesian basket holds files in style—and can be carried around when necessary. Stationery is organized in plastic trays from an office supply store.** RIGHT: **Metro shelving under the stair offers a sleek storage solution. The entire arrangement sits on top of a polished concrete floor accented at the entrance with a slate inset.**

When chef and cookbook author Evan Kleiman bought her Spanish-style house in Los Angeles, she initially wanted to rip out the concrete backyard and turn the space into a garden. Advised that this could weaken the structure of her house and its adjoining garage, making them more vulnerable to earthquake damage, she instead transformed the area into a lush container garden.

In the 1960s, the garage had undergone a less-than-tasteful renovation, becoming a knotty-pine-paneled "rec room" for teenagers. Knowing that the building would make a perfect home office, Evan hired architect Michele Saee to oversee an update.

In the former garage that is now Evan's office, a mosaic of kilim rugs and a large urn of sunflowers beckon beyond the pivoting window-door. OPPOSITE: The curving birch wall is an understated yet memorable architectural element. Its warm golden-green color complements the ruddy desk and credenza. Lighting installed above the wall reflects off the ceiling, while sunlight shines through the large doors.

Michele's plan allowed for a relatively inexpensive rehab. First, he ripped up the linoleum, revealing the original concrete floor beneath, which he restored, sealed and waxed. Then, to make the 22'-by-20', 440-square-foot space seem larger, he molded a curved backboard of birch plywood to stand behind Evan's desk and credenza. He stained the plywood a deep green-gold, then strung lights along the top to reflect off the ceiling and indirectly onto the desk. Evan

bought the desk not only for its color but also for its deep overhang, which gives her ample room to work with an assistant. Her credenza, made of the same wood, stores papers and office supplies and displays first-edition copies of her most recent books, including *Cucina Fresca* and *Cucina Rustica*.

The focal point of the room is a pair of huge, seven-foot-square framed glass panes that pivot on a central axis and serve as both windows and doors. Evan's desk is angled to take advantage of the light and breezes from both.

Because Evan travels extensively to research recipes for her books and for her restaurant, Cafe Angeli, collecting has become a passion. Among the treasures she showcases in her office are two large ceramic urns from Italy and copper trays and kilim rugs from Morocco. Delighted with her idyllic work environment, Evan credits Michele with the results. "With two large gestures—the door and the curved wall—this space was transformed," Evan declares. "It's nothing fancy, but it allows me to work out here in a beautiful setting. Being in the middle of the garden is my therapy."

LEFT: **A second window-door frames a view of the garden. In a variation on the standard sliding door, this one swivels on an axis.** TOP RIGHT: **Creeping fig, a prolific and hearty vine that Evan planted four years ago, now completely covers the stucco building. Funky garden furniture and a table made from a slab of granite form an outdoor seating area.** RIGHT: **An overhang in the front of the desk enables Evan and her assistant to work together.**

Cynthia Lute knows how to make things look beautiful—be it a textile, garden, kitchen, or home office. Having trained in fine arts with a focus on textile design, she pursued a career designing the fabrics used inside airplanes. As her work evolved, she found herself becoming more interested in garden design and residential interiors.

Cynthia and her husband live in a house outside Seattle that overlooks the Puget Sound. After planning its gardens, she found the setting so inviting that she decided to work at home. Constructing a new building for a garage and a home office across a courtyard from the house solved the problem of location. The entrance to the new building alludes to the architecture of the house: French doors mirror those of the kitchen.

Cynthia confesses that her aesthetic sensibility and a particular affection for art and objects from Asia prevailed over practical concerns. For example, a Chinese pharmaceutical cabinet is used for storage: its 71 drawers stash the myriad small office items that might otherwise get lost in the shuffle.

ABOVE: **The iron gate and the detailing on the exterior of the garage give it the feeling of a French farmhouse. With its exotic fish, the pool provides a tranquil stopping place** between home and office. OPPOSITE: **For Cynthia, no surface is complete without something from her garden. The old wooden table adds to the casual country atmosphere, while a** wooden chair, with its faintly **painted angel's face, is a bit more mysterious. Paint brushes rest in assorted pots and pitchers, next to carpet samples and sketches.**

One corner of the office is reserved for relaxation and can double as a guest room. Doors from a theater in Singapore were refashioned into screens to guarantee privacy in this area, which Cynthia outfitted with an 18th-century French daybed and an old porcelain bathtub and sink.

LEFT: **A busy home office can quickly become cluttered with lots of odds and ends. Cynthia keeps hers sorted in a 17th-century Chinese pharmaceutical cabinet which does the job beautifully.**
RIGHT: **Cynthia sometimes does her writing and telephoning while stretched out on a French daybed.**

Timothy left the city behind in more ways than one when he created his home office up the hill from his house. OPPOSITE: The magical garden setting and sweeping views of the Pacific inspire Timothy on a daily basis.

Route 1 narrows as it winds north of San Francisco through the hills. On the ascent to Bolinas, where views of the Pacific below are breathtaking, the drama increases. No signs exist to point the way; one just has to know how to get there. It is in this bucolic outpost that Timothy Maxson has chosen to live and work.

When Timothy began construction on his getaway house in Bolinas, he still ran a catering and special events business in the city. Once he decided to move full-time to the country, he transferred his accounts and his event-consulting company to his home office.

Set in a field of lavender, black bamboo, and olive trees, a charming 14'-by-11', 154-square-foot cottage up a hill from the main residence houses the office. Budget was key to Timothy's plan—in fact, he executed the entire job using low-priced materials, recycled furniture, and paint. He fabricated walls out of rough-sawn plywood panels studded with slim battens. Over their rustic surface, he layered thin glazes of a rich ocher-mustard hue that he finds uplifting even on the foggiest of days. The floor, too, is plywood, painted a pale, warm coral.

ABOVE: **An old repainted table acts as a printer stand.**
RIGHT: **Colorful vases capture the light from Timothy's garden. Cards, memos, and personal photos cover an old-fashioned bulletin board.**

Fully cognizant of how costly windows can be, Timothy canvased about 20 stores until he found a set of Marvin casement windows that had been ordered by someone else and never picked up. He purchased them at less than one-quarter their retail value. A pair of skylights and double French doors leading out to a deck supplement the light from the casements.

Once Timothy had established the background for his office, he recycled a collection of tables to hold his books and supplies. The printer connected to his laptop sits on an old oak cabinet he painted gold.

Despite his budget consciousness, Timothy realized he should invest in a comfortable office chair to pull up to the recycled wood table he uses as a desk. He chose a model that swivels and rolls, so he can maneuver around the room with ease.

OPPOSITE: **Timothy's desk is made of recycled wood. Large terracotta planters support a plank of redwood that acts as an impromptu bookshelf. The vibrant painting by Robert Surface, a Mill Valley artist, adds to** the colorful palette.
TOP RIGHT: **A spray of wild grasses enlivens a tabletop used for telephone, electric pencil sharpener, and office materials.**
RIGHT: **Fennel, wildflowers, and herbs create a rustic tableau.**

Most weekends throughout the year, Rodolfo Machado and Jorge Silvetti retreat to Wellfleet on Cape Cod. Jorge, who is chairman of the Architecture Department at the Graduate School of Design at Harvard University, and Rodolfo, a professor-in-practice of architecture and urban design, both agreed that a second home would offer them a respite from their whirlwind schedule of traveling, lecturing, and teaching—even if they occasionally ended up working there to meet their deadlines.

During the two-hour drive from their Boston office to Cape Cod, the landscape changes dramatically, from crowded streets to verdant wetlands, indigenous marsh grasses, and black pines. This is the setting for their 13-by-15-foot home office, located within a diminutive outbuilding shrouded by a wooded glade at the edge of their property. Although government regulations forbid construction on the cape's wetlands, a grandfather clause allowed a new building to rise on the footprint of an existing structure—in this case, a small garage.

For the sake of continuity, the men, both internationally acclaimed architects, incorporated the pines surrounding the building into their design. Six peeled

The home office sits in an outbuilding on the edge of a pine-bordered marsh: at high tide water surrounds it on three sides. OPPOSITE: **The tree trunks incorporated into the entryway are an integral part of the design, repeated as columns inside. The front and back doors are in perfect alignment, affording a view straight through. The interior is kept as simple as possible: twin drafting tables are each paired with a Thonet chair from the 1940s recovered in purple velvet.**

trunks define the structure—two at the entrance, two on the back porch, and two inside. As Rodolfo describes it, the trees "skewer" the house, and also create a "promenade" from front to back.

Together, Rodolfo and Jorge applied their expertise to crafting a simple, symmetrical interior that graciously accommodates their twin drafting tables and a sleeping loft for weekend visitors. The loft, which protrudes over the back porch section, also supports the roof in the truss-free structure. The remaining space in the otherwise spartan setting was assigned to a pair of wicker Lloyd Loom chairs and a small oak table holding a few personal mementos, a '50s lamp, and, of course, the fax machine.

OPPOSITE LEFT: **Continuing the symmetry of the interior, two benches sit on either side of the back porch. Sea breezes drift in through the bay window** to the sleeping loft above.

OPPOSITE RIGHT: **A 1950s metal lamp, personal knickknacks, a figure of Nipper, and the ever-essential fax machine all share** space on an old wooden table.

ABOVE: **Drafting tables aside, this is still the country: a hammock beckons beyond the back porch.**

Unencumbered by tradition, quixotic home offices are distinguished by their daring and their ingenuity. For home owners who value self-expression above pragmatism, these offices reflect the strong belief that an efficient work space can

also be offbeat, witty, and unconventional.

Many such offices

can be found in un-expected places—a 300-year-old haci-enda, a tent in Idaho, a houseboat—yet all offer invaluable

lessons in the art of blending contem-porary business equipment with antiques, personal me-mentos, or flea-market finds.

CHAPTER 7

QUIXOTIC SOLUTIONS

In Taos, New Mexico, the sunlight is so intense that when it illuminates Ray Trotter's 300-year-old adobe hacienda, it is as if a postcard had come to life. Originally a Spanish fort, Ray's building retains most of its original elements—a testament to the durability of the indigenous architecture of the Southwest. The ceilings with their primitive, hand-hewn *vigas,* the *kiva* fireplaces modeled from the same adobe as the walls, and the floors, handcrafted from a rudimentary mixture of mud and straw cured with ox blood, are all authentic.

When the opportunity arose to buy the venerable building, Ray, a nationally known expert on the art and culture of the Southwest, decided to relocate both his gallery, R. B. Ravens, and his home. In this unique spot, he could showcase antique Navajo, Pueblo, and Hispanic textiles as well as pottery, jewelry, and paintings by the Taos Founding Artists. Reserving the back of the house for living space, he exhibits the art in the front rooms facing the plaza. By carving a passageway through the walls, Ray linked two sections of the old fort, creating a 20'-by-10', 200-square-foot office in-between. The arrangement allows Ray to indulge in one of his favorite pastimes—admiring the gallery when it's closed.

Beyond Ray's 300-year-old hacienda and its arcaded gallery stands the Taos church made famous by artist Georgia O'Keeffe.
BELOW: **Authentic Pueblo vessels are put to practical use.** OPPOSITE: **Elegant and sculptural in and of itself, the stepped adobe wall has no need for decorations. Navajo blankets dating from the 1930s fill a wooden armoire. Through the doorway, Ray's antique partners desk sits below assorted wall hangings.**

Respecting the authenticity of the architecture, Ray made no structural alterations to the room. He merely furnished it with cherished pieces he had collected over the years, such as an early 1900s partners desk he found in Paris, Texas, and an old judge's chair from New Mexico. Shelving units made of natural pine boards hold books, research materials, and catalogs.

Lighting was the only major issue for Ray—a self-proclaimed pencil-and-paper man. The room has a skylight but only one small window, so he decided that track lighting was a necessary evil. His need to update the office for efficiency's sake was secondary to his commitment to maintaining the authenticity of the space and operating within that framework, so he calculated his precise needs, then strategically placed as few lamps as possible alongside the *vigas*.

LEFT: **Colorful votives brighten the mantle above the glowing** *kiva* **fireplace. The scent of sage incense fills the air. Behind the desk, ceiling-high pine bookcases hold catalogs, portfolios, and books. The turn-of-the-century wooden bench is from New Mexico.** BELOW: **With the exception of yellow legal pads and a phone, none of the trappings of a modern office are visible on top of Ray's antique partners desk (the fax is kept in the gallery). His treasures —paintings, pottery, and wall hangings—take center stage. A bronze lamp with a turn-of-the-century parchment shade casts a glow on the work at hand.**

ABOVE & OPPOSITE: **Hannah's eight-sided canvas "tent" has a cedar-shake roof and a stone floor that extends to a long deck overlooking the lake.** BELOW: **Hannah sometimes works with her television scripts and storyboards spread out around her on the bed.**

Although freelance television director Hannah Hempstead's home base is Los Angeles, she prefers to head north—to a small town called Hope, in the hills of Idaho, and to the quirky getaway she created for herself there.

Captivated by a magazine article about unusually designed canvas tents, Hannah thought that some version of such a tent might be the perfect solution for her plot of land. With the help of friends, she built a platform to lift the tent off the ground, then laid an octagonal floor of local stone on top, and constructed a frame out of trunks cut from trees on the property. Noah Kienholz, a friend of Hannah's who builds sets for television productions, helped her design and fabricate the canvas tent. With its multiple flaps, zippers, and screens, the tent is a cloistered, cozy hideaway. A cedar-shake roof protects the structure.

Hannah transformed the interior into a mini-vacation home and office. Furnishing the tent proved the most entertaining part of the project. A search through cartons of items gathered over the years yielded an intriguing mixture of "found objects": one painted

ABOVE: **A rolling rattan cabinet fits in perfectly with the rustic decor. Antique thermos jugs line up along the overhead shelf and a hanging shoe bag cleverly organizes everything from flyswatters to stationery.**

RIGHT: **An umbrella positioned outside the window functions as an awning—filtering the hot midday sunlight.**

ABOVE: **Hannah's rustic bed was made by a local artist.**
OPPOSITE LEFT: **Hannah's penchant for funky and primitive objects explains the presence of the Underwood portable typewriter—the laptop of its day!** OPPOSITE TOP RIGHT: **A curious mixture of "found objects" decorates the office.** OPPOSITE BOTTOM RIGHT: **An antique wooden box as big as a trunk functions as a desk drawer. Its compartment tray contains a calculator, FedEx envelopes, colored markers—all the necessities of backwoods life.**

wooden box stores supplies and doubles as a table, while other rough-hewn tables, piled with books, hold candlesticks used for lighting.

Crafted from local trees, the rustic bed, topped with a futon mattress and covered with an antique quilt, is Hannah's favorite place to spread out storyboards when she's working on the nuts and bolts of one of her commercials.

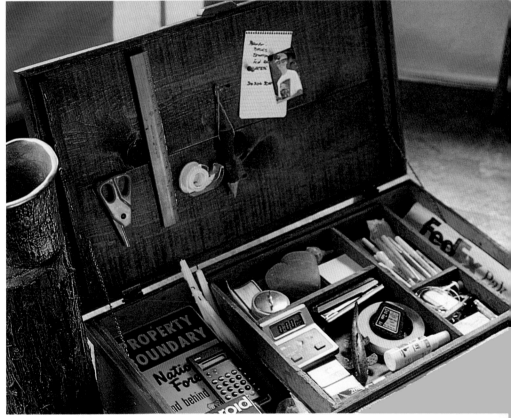

The founder and director of the Young-Malin Archive in New York City is an expert on the Surrealist artists who fled Europe for New York during the Second World War. The archival material she has amassed over the past 20 years includes correspondence, vintage and contemporary photographs, books, films, taped interviews, and even some original works by prominent artists of the movement.

Flexibility and efficiency were key issues in planning a home office to accommodate her still-growing archives. In keeping with the spirit of the Surrealists, whose art

An "eye" within the "ear" peeks into the inner office. FAR RIGHT: The elliptical-shaped office incorporates a recessed wall section which acts as a small "display window" for photographs currently under research. A small sketch of Cocteau hangs from the wooden pillar.

often depicted body parts out of context, architect Steven Alton developed a unique design based on the shape of an ear—an appropriate reflection of the owner's role as "listener and recorder" of the Surrealist movement. While focusing on the more "playful aspects of the Surrealists' art," this imaginative space ultimately mirrors the work that is done at the archive.

Metal artist Fran Taubman acid-washed, lacquered, and waxed industrial-grade rusted steel panels, then bolted them together to create the organic form of an ear. When viewed close-up, the individual panels look like abstract paintings. Small openings dot the "ear," allowing the owner to peer out into the larger space. The 7-foot-high, 10-foot-diameter structure stands in the center of a 2,400-square-foot loft with 13-foot-high ceilings.

The owner's tools of the trade—in addition to her role as archivist, she writes and lectures—are a computer, printer, and fax. All are harbored within the structure of the ear, as is an area for meetings with the academics, graduate students, publishers, and filmmakers who consult the archive.

A simple laminate desktop and a series of low bookshelves follow the inside curve of the ear. Midway around the curve, the work surface drops to an extension that serves as a small conference table. Standard-issue metal file cabinets fit neatly under-

OPPOSITE: **The office is nestled within a semicircle of steel panels. The curves of the desk and bookshelves give the room a cocoon-like quality. While a ledge supports the printer and fax, a laptop computer allows the owner some mobility within the small space. On the table extension, a pair of limited-edition shoes designed by Pierre Cardin in homage to Magritte adds to the Surrealist atmosphere.** ABOVE: **In addition to the natural light from the large windows, recessed lighting and gooseneck lamps attached to the tops of the bookshelves illuminate the office. An assortment of decorative hands stands in front of file boxes covered with hand-marbled paper.**

A closer view of the exterior walls of the "ear" reveals variations in the color and texture of the acid-washed, lacquered, and waxed industrial-grade steel panels. The shelving unit is from Zero Design.

RIGHT: Snake-like halogen lamps can be adjusted to target specific work areas. A metal "easel" below the window opening is used to prop up books and papers.

neath. Snake-like halogen lamps screwed to the tops of the bookcases target specific work zones.

Surrounding the outer ear, a system of floor-to-ceiling shelving units from Zero Design are installed against the brick walls of the loft. Their resemblance to scaffolding reminds the owner of the Surrealists' fascination with American design—particularly with the superstructure of the Brooklyn Bridge and the technology that enabled skyscrapers to rise ever higher above New York City.

ABOVE: **The stone tower rises between two shingled cottages. The rough fieldstone of the base anchors the windowed octagonal lookout.** RIGHT: **A mission-style desk complements the spareness of the beautiful wooden floors in the second story computer room.** OPPOSITE: **The handrail of the custom-designed spiral stair is made from an exhaust pipe; the posts are aluminum and the central shaft is stainless steel.**

Blake Bichanich, an associate in a busy Minneapolis architectural firm, works part of the time from a complex consisting of two small turn-of-the-century cottages and the newly constructed tower that links them on Long Lake, a half-hour drive from downtown.

For the tower's unique form, Blake drew inspiration from two types of structures he admires: the silo and the lighthouse. Constructed of local fieldstone, the tower rises 40 feet high, tapering from a diameter of 16 feet at its base to 12 feet at the crown. A metal stair spirals through the center of the tower to connect its three levels.

The ground floor can be entered from the outside as well as from Blake's living room in one of the cottages. It is spare and serene, its only furnishings a large drafting table, a turn-of-the-century chair, an original 1960s chair upholstered in faux leopard, and a 1920s chaise Blake purchased from a local farmer for $5.00 when he was just 12 years old.

Blake designated the second story for work at the computer. He placed a mission-style oak desk near a window so he could gaze out over the lake. His printer and fax keep him in touch with the Minneapolis office .

The ascent to the octagonal, windowed room on the third level lets Blake shift gears. Designed for reading, thinking, or meditating, the light-filled space encourages relaxation. The tower's archetypal form gives it a distinct identity, yet it is an integral part of the rest of the house. This was Blake's aim. "I wanted to remain connected to the house," he explains, "but I needed that sense of enclosure. The tower is my space."

Suzanne Lipschutz, a self-professed "unstoppable collector," is the founder and longtime owner of Second Hand Rose, a SoHo, New York City, shop specializing in decorative arts from 1860 to 1905. The shop, an outgrowth of her habit of finding unique, offbeat, and interesting items—even "stuff from the street"—is thriving.

This same unerring eye for the unusual led Suzanne to buy her second home, a late 1920s, Spanish-style, three-bedroom house in the Art Deco district of Miami's South Beach. Her aim was to move back and forth between New York and the "Villa Lipschutz," all the while remaining linked to her shop by telephone and Federal Express.

Suzanne wanted a tropical paradise retreat as an antidote to her fast-paced life in New York, and she got it. Her Mediterranean-style "Villa Lipshutz" in Miami is surrounded by palm trees and exotic flowers.
RIGHT: Every piece is one of a kind in Suzanne's home office. Treasured objects sit on Burmese carved shelves. The 1920s desk from Syria is made of inlaid bone, ivory, and mother-of-pearl. Suzanne embedded seashells from the beach into the pigmented stucco walls.

The transformation of a small, 250-square-foot, 14'-by-18' former "Florida room" off the house's courtyard speaks to Suzanne's ingenuity. Ripping away tired drywall, she uncovered stucco. To enhance its Mediterranean appearance, she rubbed a high-gloss, coral-hued pigment into the stucco, then encrusted the surface with tendrils of seashells. Once the walls were prepared, she removed plywood and glass panes

from the previously boarded-up windows to create openings in the walls similar to those found in Moroccan homes, allowing air to flow freely to interior rooms.

The decor of Suzanne's home office might best be described as Morocco meets Miami: the seashell-embellished walls, tile floors, and kilim rugs form an exuberantly eclectic backdrop for Suzanne's collections. Needless to say, standard office furniture would not fit into Suzanne's world. Instead, an exotic Syrian desk dating from the 1920s is teamed with a pair of late-19th-century American Gothic Revival lamps and a curvy, high-backed, 1910 Arts and Crafts wooden chair from Scotland. An authentic Mediterranean house could not function without a courtyard, and neither could Suzanne's, so she carved off some space from the office and converted it into a trellis-covered "shade room" for her orchids.

OPPOSITE: **Looking through a window into Suzanne's colorful office is like catching a glimpse of an ever-changing kaleidoscope. The tropical flowers that fill the room are all homegrown. A bed covered with Victorian lace is reserved for guests.** ABOVE: **One of Suzanne's favorite places to work is outside at the tile and stone table.**

A mix of materials and colors enlivens a windowless basement office. The sensuous curved lines of the Noguchi lamp and the brushed steel legs of the desk soften the edges of the room. Metro shelving along the wall stores stationery, catalogs, and the fax machine.

When Masa and Dava Muramatsu first opened Eastern Accent, their intimate home-accessory shop on Newbury Street in Boston, they also lived above it, in a small 400-square-foot apartment. When at last they moved to a house in Sudbury, a small town west of Boston, Masa transferred the wholesale division of the business to their home and began working out of a new office he set up in the basement. Dava, who continues to commute, remains responsible for the retail shop.

Because it had already been divided into several finished rooms, one of which measured 10 by 12 feet, the basement was large enough to suit Masa's work style. In keeping with a Japanese belief that color can promote energy and inspiration, and intrigued by its ability to transform space, Masa and Dava painted the walls a sunny golden tone they call "fiesta." "We brought nature inside," says Masa. "By using color, texture, and shape, we infused the room with a totally different feeling, making it bright and uplifting." Wainscoting made from wood planks salvaged from a barn was left untouched, and an old carpet was ripped up to reveal a concrete floor, which the couple cleaned and waxed.

LEFT: **Comfortable pillows and beautiful ceramics define the Muramatsus' "non-work" area.** RIGHT: **A long calligraphy scroll made by Masa's mother further personalizes the space. On the filing cabinet sit two clocks, one set to Massachusetts time, the other to Japanese. A black wooden screen strategically camouflages the heater.** BOTTOM RIGHT: **Galvanized steel drawers organize office supplies. This set, made in Japan, is lightweight and won't rust.**

Masa set aside one corner of the room, marking it off with four large Japanese pillows—called *zabuton*—and a sisal rug, to inspire "creativity and energy flow." Here he indulges in non-work-related activities, such as reading, drawing, meditating, or taking a break to spend time with the couple's daughter, Aya.

Lighting was brought into the windowless space in the form of a sculptural, 6-foot-tall Isamu Noguchi lamp; another, smaller Noguchi creation sits on the floor. A gooseneck-style lamp serves to light the desk—a maple table with curved steel legs that was stained with an olive-hued finish. Storage is minimal: a file cabinet, some black Metro shelving, and a galvanized metal box with drawers. A dehumidifier controls any basement moisture.

Everything about Tara Solomon and her Miami Beach home office is unique. Call her answering machine, for instance, and you'll hear "You've reached the glamorous home office of Tara Solomon." Tara covers the South Beach social scene for *The Miami Herald* and is a contributor to *Elle* and *In Style*. Always on the go, this high-energy writer is also developing her own web site.

Tara's 900-square-foot, one-bedroom apartment overlooking Biscayne Bay from the ninth floor of one of Miami's 1960s high-rises is a shrine to the marriage of retro and avant-garde. In her 17'-by-23' office, which

LEFT: **Where modern is retro— that's Miami. Tara's work area occupies one end of the living room in her apartment. The funky wrought iron chair is by local artist Carlos Bettencourt.** RIGHT: **Just another day at the office for Tara, dressed in vintage Pucci—of course!**

occupies the windowed end of her living room, chubby chartreuse Vladimir Kagan club chairs from the 1960s, a hanging George Nelson parchment globe lamp, and a 1950s metal school desk team up with contemporary art purchased from local Miami artists.

Tara sees her eclectic decor as the antidote to her former day job, where she felt victimized by having to work in a sterile, windowless room under the glare of fluorescent lights. When she was finally able to dictate the identity of her own space, she opted for color and dazzle—painting the walls a cheerful orange and warming her floor with a leopard-print rug.

Tara's home office integrates well with the rest of the living room, but when she needs to hide the clutter on the shelves behind her desk, she uses a screen she commissioned from local artist Joseph Seeman. Each of the screen's vivid, boldly painted panels depicts women at work, a subject close to Tara's heart.

While her spray-painted desk and mermaid lamp might seem out of synch with her state-of-the-art lineup of fax, phone, computer, and ergonomic keyboard, the offbeat items please her and mix well with a work environment that suits her style perfectly.

OPPOSITE TOP LEFT: **Tara's command post: a 1950s school desk spray painted and further decorated with pink glass beads. A mermaid looks down from her lamp at all the activity.**

OPPOSITE BOTTOM LEFT: **Where would a society writer be without her power Rolodex? Tara keeps 3,000 names on hand, organized and color-coded by category. Quirky stationery reflects her personality, and an ergonomic keyboard from Microsoft lessens the pressure from writing every day on deadline.**

LEFT: **The office overlooks sparkling Biscayne Bay.**

A sense of rugged individualism prevails among the owners of the houseboats that line the docks of Seattle's Lake Union. For five of these pioneers, this individualism extends to their home offices, all masterminded by architect and neighbor Gene Morris.

Gene and his wife Margaret, an interior designer, maintain offices outside their home, but find that the one Gene tucked into their 12'-by-16' bedroom under the eaves of their houseboat comes in handy on weekends and evenings as well as when their small daughter is out of school. The office, which the couple shares, consists primarily of a maple-topped table. An additional slab of maple drops down in front of the table to function as the headboard for their bed, and a second table, pushed up against the wall, holds their computer.

LEFT: **Gene Morris, a member of the houseboat community of Lake Union in Seattle, takes his morning coffee outdoors.** RIGHT: **Houseboat life means not wasting an inch of space. The Morrises' desk doubles as a headboard for the bed. A computer table off to the side extends the work area into an L-shape.**

Arlene Hills, a massage therapist, lives just a few steps away from the Morrises. When she saw Gene's setup, she requested something equally compact for her own houseboat. What she got was a 4'-by-6' pine cabinet purchased at Abodio, a Seattle furniture shop. The piece fits neatly under the stairwell leading to the second level of her boat. Its double doors open to reveal compartments of varying sizes, which hold everything from pens to a computer. There is also a desktop that folds out like a Murphy bed, plus sliding shelves for the computer keyboard and a fax machine.

OPPOSITE: **Arlene Hills, another houseboat dweller, keeps her office in a pine cupboard. The doors open to reveal sliding drawers, compartments, and file cabinets. A collapsible table folds out into a desk.** TOP: **Arlene's home looks more house than boat, particularly when a small launch pulls up to the dock.** BOTTOM: **At quitting time, Arlene's home office simply folds up into an unobtrusive pine armoire.**

Surain and Robert afSandeberg, who recently completed a major renovation of their houseboat, also hired Gene as architect. Incorporated into the design was a home office for Surain, who is financial manager for the Nature Conservancy of Washington. While Robert commutes by kayak across the lake to his job at a computer company, Surain stays at home, at least part-time, to work on her projects.

Gene situated the office—which, at 120 square feet within a 9'-by-13' space, is large by houseboat standards—on the second level. A doorway leads out to a deck and hot tub—perfect for work breaks on stressful days. Inside, the office is airy and bright. The desk, an 8-foot-long slab of maple straddling a pair of black file cabinets, is positioned to take advantage of the lake view. An area dedicated to open shelving accommodates storage needs. Surain and Robert met in Nepal and continue to travel extensively, so it's fitting that the office is filled with pottery and indigenous crafts from various exotic locales.

OPPOSITE: **The afSandebergs' office is on the second level of their houseboat. The couple share an 8-foot-long desk, where Robert uses an ergonomic "posture chair" from Sweden.** TOP: **The storage closet uses fabric in lieu of a door—an inexpensive and attractive solution. File organizers and storage boxes from IKEA keep papers neat. Pottery from Chile, Peru, and Southeast Asia shares a shelf with the fax machine.** BOTTOM: **The office windows are visible from under the peaked roof of the afSandebergs' houseboat.**

ACKNOWLEDGMENTS

I'd like to begin by saying a most sincere thank you to my agent, Doe Coover. Without Doe and her endless support, it would not have been possible for me to do this book. Her insight, wisdom, and humor helped carry me through this project from start to finish.

I am especially grateful to Grey Crawford for his beautiful photography, and for bringing a level of commitment to this project that is rare. Heartfelt thanks to Janet Tashjian for keeping me on track on a daily basis while writing the text. A debt of gratitude also to Christopher Phillips, who pitched in during the final days of writing and gave of his time and talents. Thanks also to Bo Niles for her talents as text editor.

I am truly fortunate to have worked with the amazing team at Artisan. Sincere thanks to my publisher, Leslie Stoker, for her support and insight, and to Jim Wageman, whose creative talents as art director made this such a beautiful book. Special thanks also to editor Siobhán McGowan, for her fine-tuning, to Christina Sheldon, for being so accommodating, and to Alexandra Maldonado and Hope Koturo, for their professional support. The same gratitude goes to Beth Wareham—I am very lucky to have her as a publicist.

And, of course, I am forever indebted to all those who graciously opened up their homes to us. Without their generosity, this book certainly would not exist. Deepest thanks to all of you.

The talented staff at *Metropolitan Home* has always been invaluable to me—that was especially true while researching this book. Thanks to Donna Warner, Arlene Hirst, Newell Turner, and Linda O'Keefe. *Met Home* City Editors Linda Humphrey, Diane Saeks, Mindy Pantiel, and Pam Hait were extremely helpful, as were Victoria Lautman, Susan Weinberger, and Rima Suqi. Special thanks to Barbara Thornburg for all of her time.

Thanks to David Akiba, who believed in me long before this book, and who was an inspiring mentor. To Sara Giovanitti, who many years ago gave her support to me—thank you.

I was so fortunate to form many new friendships during this process, and I offer my sincere thanks to all of you who invited me to stay in your homes: Stephen Gibson, Randy Whitehead, John Maienza, Nick and Deb Berman, Steven Wagner, Christina Davila and Bob Brodsky, Pam and Glen Hait, Elaine Paul, Gail and Joe Anthony, Mario Villa, Meg and Peter Strattner, and Victoria Darrow. Thanks also to Leslie Tweeton at the Arizona Biltmore, Serge Denis at the Meridien Hotel Boston, and Jennifer, Jason, and Mera Rubell at the Greenview Hotel in Miami for their support and generosity. Thanks also to Meredith Post and the folks at the Kimpton Group who made sure I was comfortable at their wonderful hotels: the Beverly Prescott in Los Angeles, the Monaco and the Triton in San Francisco and the Vintage Park in Seattle. Thanks also go out to my fabulous travel agent Deborah Crockett, for handling my complex travel arrangements. Patty Tucker at American Airlines also provided considerable assistance.

Heartfelt thanks to all my dear friends and colleagues who gave their time, advice, feedback, and support throughout this project: Dylan Landis, Barbara Graustark, Karen Kurlander, Cheryl and Jeffrey Katz, Stephen Gibson, Carolyn Sagov, Wally Higgins, Gail Eisenkraft, Marilyn Hafner, Fred Bernstein, Sarah and Andy Spongberg, Antonio Da Motta Leal, Maynard Lyndon, Bridget Eckland, Donna Sapolin, Dava and Masa Muramatsu, Mili Bermejo and Dan Greenspan, David Mullman, Martha Labell, Karen Fisher, Mike Strohl, Chris Madden, David Staskowski, Olga Bravo, Becky Wagner, Tim McTague, Barry Kucker. It meant so much to me.

ABODIO
217 Pine Street, Suite 200
Seattle, Washington 98101
206·343·3030
desks, chairs, lighting, storage, accessories

ARROYO DESIGN
224 North Fourth Avenue
Tucson, Arizona 85705
602·884·1012
desks, storage

ARTEMIDE LIGHTING
200 Lexington Avenue
New York, New York 10016
212·685·6556
lighting

ASHER BENJAMIN & COMPANY
Distributed by Harden Furniture
Mill Pond Way
McConnellsville, New York 13401
315·245·1000
lighting

BALDINGER REPRESENTATIVES
Enterprise Lighting
110 Greene Street, Suite 501
New York, New York 10012
212·343·9300
lighting

BENJAMIN MOORE & COMPANY
51 Chestnut Ridge Road
Montvale, New Jersey 07645
800·826·2623
paint, painting supplies

NICK BERMAN DESIGN
1301 Tigertail Road
Los Angeles, California 90049
310·476·6242
storage

BOYD LIGHTING
944 Folsom Street
San Francisco, California 94107-1007
415·778·4300
lighting

BROYHILL FURNITURE INDUSTRIES, INC.
One Broyhill Park
Lenoir, North Carolina 28633
800-327-6944
desks

CRATE & BARREL
Administrative Offices
725 Landwehr Road
Northbrook, Illinois 60062
847·272·2888
desks, storage, accessories

DA MOTTA STUDIO
295 Park Avenue South, Apartm
New York, New York 10010
212·995·2201
storage

DAVIS FURNITURE INDUSTRIES, INC.
2401 South College Drive
P.O. Box 2065
High Point, North Carolina 27261-2065
336·910·889·2009
desks, storage

DELTA ACCESS USA INC.
8182 Maryland Avenue, Suite 806
Clayton, Montana 63105
800·327·3589
storage

[handwritten notes: DAVID BURROUGHS, LTD 410·785·1976 Karen will send info. 6·19·98]

Delta Stationery Module

DETAILS
214 Durham Drive
Athens, Alabama 35611
800·833·0411
lighting, accessories

DIMENSIONS STORAGE SYSTEMS
533 Stone Road, Unit D
Benicia, California 94510
800·225·3772
storage

DOMAIN
938 Broadway
New York, New York 10010
212·228·7450
desks, chairs, storage, accessories

DOOR STORE
1201 Third Avenue
New York, New York 10021
212·772·1110
desks, chairs, storage

DREXEL HERITAGE
FURNISHINGS, INC.
101 North Main Street
Drexel, North Carolina 28619
800·447·4700
desks, chairs

EGAN VISUAL
300 Hanlan Road
Woodbridge, Ontario L4L3P6
CANADA
800·263·2387 (IN US)
800·263·2316 (IN CANADA)
storage, accessories

ETHAN ALLEN
Ethan Allen Drive
P.O. Box 1966
Danbury, Connecticut 06813-1966
800·228·9229
desks, chairs, storage

FLOS
200 McKay Road
Huntington Station, New York 11746
516·549·2745
lighting

FURNITURE AT WORK
517 South Lamar Boulevard
Austin, Texas 78704
512·445·7001
desks, chairs, lighting, storage, accessories

GREEN FURNITURE COMPANY
267 Commercial Street
Portland, Maine 04101
207·775·4234
desks, storage

H 2 B COMPANY
610 22nd Street, Suite 247
San Francisco, California 94107
800·829·6580
accessories

HAWORTH, INC.
One Haworth Center
Holland, Michigan 49423-9576
616·393·3000
desks, storage

HEKMAN FURNITURE COMPANY
1400 Buchanan Southwest
Grand Rapids, Michigan 49507
616·452·1411
desks, chairs

HERMAN MILLER FOR THE HOME
855 East Main Street
Zeeland, Michigan 49464-0302
616·654·3000
desks, chairs, lighting, storage, accessories

HUNTER DOUGLAS
2 Park Way & Route 17 South
Upper Saddle River, New Jersey 07458
201·327·8200
accessories

IKEA
East Coast
1000 Center Drive
Elizabeth, New Jersey 07202
908·289·4488
800·434·4532 (phone orders)
desks, chairs, lighting, storage, accessories

IKEA
West Coast
17621 East Gale Avenue
City of Industry, California 91748
818·912·4532
desks, chairs, lighting, storage, accessories

JANOVIC PLAZA PAINT
159 West 72nd Street
New York, New York 10023
212·595·2500
paint, painting supplies

KNOLL
1235 Water Street
East Greenville, Pennsylvania 18041
800·445·5045
desks, chairs, lighting, storage, accessories

KROHN ABBOTT DESIGNS
6178 West Jefferson Boulevard
Los Angeles, California 90016
310·840·5997
desks, chairs, lighting, storage, accessories

LIGNE ROSET
200 Lexington Avenue
New York, New York 10016
212·685·1099
storage

LUXO CORPORATION
36 Midland Avenue
Port Chester, New York 10573
800·222·5896
lighting

MAINE COTTAGE FURNITURE
P.O. Box 935
Yarmouth, Maine 04096
207·846·1430
desks, chairs, storage

MANES STREET
200 Lexington Avenue
New York, New York 10016
212·684·7050
desks, chairs

NORTH COAST MEDICAL, INC.
187 Stauffer Boulevard
San Jose, California 95125-1042
408·283·1900
chairs

PLACEWARES
Corporate Offices
346-R Vanderbilt Avenue
Norwood, Massachusetts 02062
617·769·8500
desks, lighting, storage, accessories

PRESSMAN DESIGN STUDIO/HOME SUITE OFFICE
271 Miller Road
East Greenbush, New York 12061
518·479·0012
desks, storage

SLIGH FURNITURE COMPANY
1201 Industrial Avenue
Holland, Michigan 49423
616·392·7101
desks, chairs, storage

STAPLES, INC.
Corporate Offices
100 Pennsylvania Avenue
Framingham, Massachusetts 01701-9328
508·370·8500
desks, chairs, lighting, storage, accessories

STEELCASE, INC.
901 44th Street
Grand Rapids, Michigan 49508
800·227·2960
desks, chairs, lighting, storage

STOREHOUSE
6368 Dawson Boulevard
Norcross, Georgia 30093
800·869·2468
desks, chairs, storage, accessories

TECHLINE
5117 University Avenue
Madison, Wisconsin 53705
800·356·8400
desks, storage

TECKNION, INC.
901 Lincoln Drive West
Marlton, New Jersey 08053
609·596·7608
desks, chairs, lighting, storage

TECKNION FURNITURE SYSTEMS
1150 Flint Road
Downsview, Ontario M3J2J5
CANADA
416·661·3370
desks, chairs, lighting, storage

**THOMASVILLE FURNITURE
INDUSTRIES, INC.**
P.O. Box 339
Thomasville, North Carolina 27361
910·472·4000
desks, chairs

TURNSTONE
A Steelcase Company
3528 Lousma Drive Southeast
Wyoming, Michigan 49548
800·227·2960
desks, chairs, lighting, accessories

VECTA
150 East 58th Street, 5th Floor
New York, New York 10155
212·832·7011
desks, chairs

VERSTEEL
P.O. Box 850
Jasper, Indiana 47547-0850
800·876·2120
desks, chairs

VITRA SEATING, INC.
149 Fifth Avenue
New York, New York 10010
800·338·4872
desks, chairs

WORKBENCH
470 Park Avenue South
New York, New York 10016
212·481·5454
desks, chairs, storage

ZERO DESIGN
560 Broadway
New York, New York 10012
212·925·3615
desks, chairs, storage

Springboard™ seating line from Steelcase Inc.'s Turnstone® brand

ALIMED CATALOG
800·225·2610
desks, chairs, lighting

THE CONTAINER STORE
800·733·3532
storage

CRATE & BARREL CATALOG
800·323·5461
desks, storage, accessories

EXPOSURES
800·222·4947
accessories

HOLD EVERYTHING
800·421·2264
desks, chairs, storage

LEVENGER CATALOG
800·544·0880
desks, lighting, accessories

MUSEUM OF MODERN ART CATALOG
800·447·6662
chairs, lighting, accessories

OFFICE DEPOT
800·685·8800
desks, chairs, lighting, storage

OFFICEMAX
800·788·8080
desks, chairs, storage

PAPER ACCESS CATALOG
800·727·3701
accessories

PAPER DIRECT, INC.
800·272·7377
accessories

POTTERY BARN
800·922·5507
accessories

QUILL
800·789·1331
desks, chairs, storage, accessories

RELIABLE HOME OFFICE
800·869·6000
desks, chairs, storage, accessories

RENOVATOR SUPPLY
800·659·2211
lighting, accessories

SAM FLAX CATALOG
212·620·3000
chairs, storage, accessories

SPIEGEL CATALOG
800·345·4500
desks, storage

STAPLES CATALOG
800·333·3330
desks, chairs, lighting, storage, accessories

Delta File Module

DESIGNED BY JIM WAGEMAN

THE TYPEFACE IN THIS BOOK IS GILL SANS,
DESIGNED BY ERIC GILL

PRINTED AND BOUND BY
ARNOLDO MONDADORI EDITORE S.P.A.
VERONA, ITALY